AF600166

THE CATHOLIC UNIVERSITY OF AMERICA
CANON LAW STUDIES
No. 343

The Time and Place of Sacred Ordination

A HISTORICAL SYNOPSIS AND A COMMENTARY

A DISSERATATION

Submitted to the Faculty of the School of Canan Law of The Catholic University of America in Partial Fulfillment of the Requirements for the Degree of Doctor of Canon Law

by the

REV. JOHN C. REISS, A.B., S.T.L., J.C.L.
Priest of the Diocese of Trenton

THE CATHOLIC UNIVERSITY OF AMERICA PRESS
WASHINGTON, D. C.
1953

NIHIL OBSTAT

JOANNES ROGGE SCHMIDT, J.C.D.

Censor Deputatus

Washingtonii, D.C., die 13 Augusti, 1953

IMPRIMATUR

✠ GEORGE W. AHR, S.T.D.

Episcopus Trentonensis

Trentonii, die 8 Septembris, 1953

PRINTED BY

NEW JERSEY'S BOYSTOWN PRESS

ARLINGTON, NEW JERSEY

TABLE OF CONTENTS

CHAPTER V

CHAPTER VI

CHAPTER VII

FOREWORD

The Church has the divinely appointed task of leading men to salvation, using the means determined by Christ. In carrying out this duty, the Church must provide ministers, who will dispense the mysteries of Christ, and who receive the power to do so through the sacrament of Holy Orders. Since the ministers stand as leaders of the people, the Church has always been aware of the tremendous harm which could result should any of these prove unworthy. Consequently, the Church has from the earliest times used the greatest caution in the conferring of Holy Orders, remembering constantly the solemn words of St. Paul to Timothy, "Do not lay hands hastily upon anyone." (I Tim., V, 22) Thus the Church enacted laws to safeguard the conferring of this sacrament, and included among these laws were those which determined the time and the place of sacred ordination. It is these laws which form the subject matter of this dissertation.

Since most laws of the Code of Canon Law are but repetitions of pre-existing laws, a survey of the origin and development of the Church's law on the time and the place for sacred ordination will be of immense importance. Not only will such a historical survey be interesting, but it will also be of service for interpreting the law as it exists today. Therefore, there are two parts in this dissertation: the first, a historical survey of the law on the time and the place for sacred ordination; and the second, a canonical commentary on the present-day law. The canonical commentary will consist of four chapters, which will treat separately the Episcopacy, the Major Orders, the Minor Orders, and Tonsure. It is to be pointed out that the discussion on the time for secred ordination will have reference to the days of the year when the various orders may be conferred, and the time of the day. The discussion of the proper place for sacred ordination will have reference to the proper territory where the various orders are to be conferred, and also to the proper place within the territory.

The writer wishes to express his gratitude to the Most Reverend George W. Ahr, Bishop of Trenton, New Jersey, for the opportunity to pursue graduate studies in Canon Law at The Catholic University of America; to the members of the Faculty of the School of Canon Law; and to all who have helped in any way in the preparation of this dissertation.

CHAPTER I

FROM APOSTOLIC TIMES UNTIL THE DECREE OF GRATIAN

From the depths of His divine knowledge and from His will to have all men be saved,[1] Jesus Christ instituted the seven sacraments. These He entrusted to the care of His church. It is not surprising, then, that the Church in its solicitude for the safeguarding of these channels of grace should develop and enact legislation regulating their administration and reception. Since this is true with regard to all the sacraments, it is but natural to find laws affecting the sacrament of Holy Orders. An endeavor will be made to trace the origin and development of those laws of the Church which deal with the time and place of sacred ordination. In the present chapter two articles will deal with these laws, the first treating of the time of sacred ordination, looking at the legislation as it grew from Apostolic times until the publication of the Decree of Gratian, and the second treating of the place of sacred ordination during the same period. The chronological order will be followed. No attempt will be made to treat separately the various orders—tonsure, the minor orders, subdiaconate, diaconate, priesthood, or episcopacy. Rather, they will be treated together, chiefly because there is a lack of historical evidence regarding the elements of time anl place in connection with the conferring of the Minor Orders and the episcopacy.

SECTION A. THE TIME FOR SACRED ORDINATION

In the history of the Church the first conferring of Holy Orders took place on a Thursday evening, when our Blessed Saviour with His solemn words, "do this in remembrance of Me",[2] both instituted the sacrament and bestowed it upon His Apostles.[3] Whether the

[1] I Tim., II, 4.

[2] Luke, XXII, 20; I. Cor., XI, 25.

[3] Council of Trent (1545-1563), Sess. XXII, *de Sacrifio Missae,* c.2—Denzinger-Bannwart-Umberg, *Enchiridion Symbolorum Definitionum et Declarationum, de Rebus Fidei et Morum* (ed. 21-23., St. Louis: Herder and Co., 1937), n. 949 (hereafter cited *Enchiridion*).

Apostles themselves ordained others on Holy Thursday is not mentioned in Sacred Scripture, nor in the writings of the early Church. In the *Acts of the Apostles*, however, there is a brief reference to the selection and ordination of Saint Paul and Saint Barnabas: "Then, having fasted and prayed and laid their hands upon them, they let them go."[4] This event and these words were used by Pope St. Leo I (440-461) in his letter to Dioscorus, Patriarch of Alexandria (444-451), to prove that ordination was conferred on Sunday.[5] Whether this was the valid conclusion to be drawn from the text is a matter of conjecture. It seems that whatever evidence there is in this passage does not definitely indicate at what time the ordinations were held. Aside from this indefinite reference to the conferring of Orders, Sacred Scripture does not give any indication as to when this sacrament should be administered.

Pope Anacletus (76?-88?—i.e. Pope Cletus) is reported to have written to all bishops in Italy and to have determined precisely that the consecration of bishops was to take place on Sunday at the hour of Tierce.[6] It is now known that this letter is spurious, and consequently it cannot be used as evidence for this early period. Despite the fact that this epistle is not authentic, it was later included in many canonical collections, such as the collection of Pseudo-Isidore (c.850),[7] of Burchard of Worms (✠1025),[8] of Anselm of Lucca

[4] Acts, XIII, 3.

[5] Epistle LXXIX — Jaffé, *Regesta Pontificum Romanorum ab condita Ecclesia ad annum post Christum natum MCXCVIII* (2.ed. by F. Kaltenbrunner (to the year 590), P. Ewald (590-882), and S. Loewenfeld (882-1198), and so referred to as JK, JE, JL.), n. 406; Mansi, *Sacrorum Counciliorum Nova et Amplissima Collectio* (53 vols. in 60, Parisiis, 1901-1927), V. 1241 (hereafter cited *Mansi*); Migne (1800-1875), *Patrologiae Cursus Completus, Series Latina* (221 vols., Parisiis, 1844-1855), LIV, 625 (hereafter cited *MPL*).

[6] Epistle II: "Ordinationes episcoporum auctoritate apostolica ab omnibus, qui in eadem fuerint provincia, episcopis sunt celebrandae. Qui simul convenientes scrutinium cum precibus, celebrent, manus cum sanctis evangeliis imponentes, dominica die, hora tertia orantes . . ."—JK, n.3; Mansi, I, 598: c. 1, D. LXXV.

[7] Epistola Anaceti Secunda, Capt. XVIII — Hinschius, *Decretales Pseudo-Isidorianae et Capitula Angilrammi* (Lipsiae, 1863), p. 75 (hereafter cited Hinschius).

[8] *Decretum*, I, 15 — *MPL*, CXL, 553.

(✠1086),[9] and of Ivo Chartres (✠1117).[10] At best the epistle of Anacletus is of value only in so far as it is quoted in any of these collections; and then, since these were not official, it only indicated what practice was in vogue when these collections were published. unless there existed another true and authentic declaration of an earlier pope or council.

In the beginning of the third century there appeared a document, a sort of Roman Ritual, which exerted great influence on later collections. It originated in the Western Church as a pseudo-apostolic document, and is known under the title of "The Apostolic Tradition of St. Hippolytus (✠235)".[11] In a brief passage it clearly stated that the consecration of a bishop was to take place on Sunday.[12] It is to be noted, however, that the "Apostolic Tradition" did not determine at which hour of the day the bishop was to be consecrated. It was observed by Dom Pierre de Puniet (1877-1941) that in this ancient document the ordination of priests and deacons followed immediately after the consecration of bishops without any new indication of days; presumably Sunday was the appointed day for all three ceremonies.[13]

There is ascribed to Pope St. Zepherinus (199-217) an epistle as written by him to all the bishops. In this letter the ordination to the priesthood and the diaconate was mentioned explicitly, but only

[9] *Anselmi, Episcopi Lucensis, Collectio Canonum una cum Collectione, iussu Instituti Savigniani,* — VI, 45 — ed. Thaner (Oeniponte, 1906-1915), p. 291 (hereafter cited Thaner).

[10] *Decretum,* V, 69 — *MPL,* CLXI, 549; *Panormia,* III, 12 — *MPL,* CLXI, 1132.

[11] Van Hove, *Commentarium Lovaniense in Codicem Iuris Canonici,* Vol. I, Tom. I, *Prolegomena* (2.ed., Mechliniae-Romae: H. Dessain, 1945), p. 125.

[12] "Episcopus ordinetur electus ... conveniet populum una cum presbyterio et his, qui praesentes fuerint episcopi, die dominica." — *Florilegium Patristicum* (edd. Bernhardus Geyer et Johannes Zellinger: 44 fasciculi, Bonnae: Sumptibus Petri Hanstein, 1911-1941): Fasciculus VII (Pars I-VIII) *Monumenta Eucharistica et Liturgica Vetustissima,* collegit notis et prolegomenis instruxit Johannes Quasten (Bonnae, 1935), p. 27.

[13] De Puniet, *The Roman Pontifical, A History and Commentary,* translated by Mildred V. Harcourt (London-New York-Toronto: Longmans, Green and Co., 1932), p. 95 (hereafter cited De Puniet).

in general terms, so that nothing definite was laid down.[14] Since very little information is derivable from the text of this letter, it is not a matter of much disappointment to learn that the letter is not authentic. But it also found a place in various later collections.[15]

Numerous statements in the lives of the popes who lived in the early centuries give rise to a question concerning the apparent practice of reserving ordinations solely to the month of December. This is a natural conclusion to draw from the *Liber Pontificalis*, which repeatedly says that such or such a pope ordained so many priests and deacons at the December ordinations. For example, it is said of Pope St. Marcellus (308-309): "Hic ordinavit XXV presbiteros in urbe Roma et II diaconos per mens. decemb.; episcopos per diversa loca XXI."[16] But the practice cannot have been so restricted as the book could lead one to suppose; its testimony must be received with caution. It tells us of certain Popes, as St. Lucius I (253-254)[17] and St. Sixtus II (257-258),[18] who only sat in the chair of Peter for a few months, that they held several ordinations in December; and attributes other December ordinations to Popes St. Eusebius (309

14 *Epistle II*: "Ordinationes presbyterorum levitarumque tempore congruo, multis coram astantibus, solemniter agite, . . ." — JK, n. 80; Mansi, I, 730; Migne (1800-1875), *Patrologiae Cursus Completus, Series Graeca* (161 vols., Parisiis, 1857-1866), X, 17 (hereafter cited *MPG*); c.3, D.LXXV.

15 Hinschius, p. 135; Burchardus, II, 3 — *MPL*, CXL, 625; Anselm, VII, 36 — Thaner, p. 378; Ivo, *Decretum*, VI, 23 — *MPL*, CLXI, 450-451 (in this the word "diaconorum" is used instead of "levitarum".).

16 *Liber Pontificalis*, XXXI — ed. Duchesne (2 vols., Paris, 1886-1892), Tome Premier, p. 164; *The Book of the Popes*, translated by Louise Ropes Loomis (New York: Columbia University Press, 1916), p. 38.

17 Liber Pontificalis, XXIII, ". . . Hic fecit ordinationes II per mens. decemb., presbiteros IV, diaconos IV; episcopos per diversa loca numero VII." — Duchesne, p. 153; *The Book of the Popes*, pp. 28-29.

Duchesne in his *notes explicatives* n. 4 writes: "Ce chiffre est évidemment faux: Lucius n'ayant siégé que huit mois, n'a pas célébré deux fois l'ordination de décembre." — p. 153.

18 *Liber Pontificalis*, XXV, ". . . Hic fecit ordinationes II per mens. decemb., presbiteros IV, diaconos VII; episcopos per diversa loca II." — Duchesne, p. 155; *The Book of the Popes*, p. 31.

Here in his *notes explicatives* n. 7 *ordinationes II per mens.* decemb., Duchesne states: "Chiffre évidemment faux, car il n'y a qu'un mois de décembre dans le durée du pontificat de Xystus II." — p. 155.

or 310),[19] and St. Mark (336),[20] in whose brief reigns no month of December fell. From this, De Puniet concluded that at all events there must have ben a tradition which favored December ordinations, and this seems confirmed by the fact that the Leonine Sacramentary placed ordinations immediately after the "fast of the tenth month."[21]

That it was not a strict and exclusive practice to hold ordinations only in December is obvious from the mention of ordinations held in February by Simplicius (468-483)[22] and Felix IV (526-530);[23] the latter is also said to have held an ordination in March, that is on the Saturday *Sitientes*. Hence, the only conclusion to be drawn from such references in the lives of the popes is that the month of December had not been established by law as the time for sacred ordination to the diaconate, the priesthood and the episcopacy; at

[19] *Liber Pontificalis,* XXII, "...Hic fecit ordinationem per mens. decemb., presbiteros XIII, diaconos III; episcopos per diversa loca numero XIV," — Duchesne, p. 167; *The Book of the Popes,* pp. 39-40.

Duchesne makes this observation: "Eusèbe n'ayant siégé que quatre mois, d'avril en août, il est impossible qu'il ait fait une ordination en décembre." — P. 167 in *notes explicatives* n. 4 *ad ordinationem per mens. decemb.*

[20] *Liber Pontificalis,* XXV, "...Hic fecit ordintiones II in urbe Roma per mens. decemb., presbyteros XXV, diaconos VI; episcopos per diversa loca XXVII." — Duchesne, p. 202; *The Book of the Popes,* pp. 72-73.

Duchesne in the *notes explicatives* n. 12, *ordin. II per mens. decemb.* says: "Bien que notre auteur attribue deux ans et huit mois à Marc, se pape n'a pas siége une année, mais huit mois seulement, de fèvrier à octobre, pas même une seule fois." — pp. 203-204.

[21] De Puniet, p. 94; *Sacramentarium Leonianum* — edited by Rev. Charles Lett Feltoe, B.D. (Cambridge: University Press, 1896), pp. 119-123; *MPL,* LV, 113-116.

[22] *Liber Pontificalis,* XLIX, "...Hic fecit ordinationes in urbe Roma III per mens. decemb. et febr., presbiteros LVIII, diaconos XI; episcopos per diversa loca LXXXVIII." — Duchesne, p. 249.

[23] *Liber Pontificalis,* LVI, "...Hic fecit ordinationes II in urbe Roma per mens. februario et martio, presbiteros LV, diaconos IV; episcopos per diversa loca XXIX." — Duchesne, p. 279.

most, this practice was but a strong tradition which suffered exceptions.[24]

It is only with the pontificate of Leo I (440-461) that the first indisputable document dealing with the time of ordination made its appearance. This Pope gave positive directions regarding the time for the conferral of Sacred Orders, but made no distinction in this respect between bishops, priests, and deacons. All alike were bound to receive their Orders on Sundays.[25] Leo, in the year 445, made this quite clear when he replied to a request of Dioscorus, Patriarch of Alexandria (444-451), who wanted to know whether Sacred Orders could be conferred on all days, or were to be conferred only at determined times. The Pope not only specified Sunday as the day

[24] Catalani (✠ca. 1757), citing Mabillon (1632-1707), set forth the following explanations for this tradition. He stated that the weather in December proved more satisfactory for easing the efforts of the ordaining prelate and those to be ordained. For, in summer, he said, the heat is most annoying in Rome, and autumn is occupied with harvesting. Furthermore, travel during Lent was not so convenient, and besides, at that time even the Popes and their ministers were busy with celebrating every day at the various station churches and with examining those to be baptized. Thus it left only December as an appropriate time. Though in and of itself this argument was of rather light weight, still it was advanced by a learned man, and so must have some value. — Catalani, *Pontificale Romanum in tres partes distributum Clementis VIII de Urbani VIII auctoritate recognitum nunc primum prolegomenis et commentariis illustratum* (2.ed., 3 vols., Parisiis, 1850-1852), Tom. I, 112 (hereafter cited *Commentarium*).

[25] St. Leo, *Epistle VI* [*ad Anastasium*]: "Cognovimus sane . . . a quibusdam fratribus solos episcopos tantum diebus dominicis ordinari, presbyteros vero et diaconos, circa quos par consecratio fieri debet, passim quolibet die dignitatem accipere, quod contra canones et traditionem Patrum usurpatio corrigenda committet." — *MPL,* LIV, 616; JK, n. 404; Thomassinus (1619-1695), *Vetus et Nova Ecclesiae Disciplina Circa Beneficia et Beneficiarios* (3 vols., Parisiis, 1691), Pars II, Lib. II, Cap. XII, n. 11 (hereafter cited *Vetus et Nova Disciplina*).

for ordaining according to the Apostolic teaching,[26] but also taught that the reason why Sunday was the most appropriate day for ordinations was that all the gifts of divine grace were bestowed on that day: "... ut quidquid a Domino est insigne constitutum, in huius diei dignitate sit gestum. In hac mundum sumpsit exordium; in hac per resurrectionem et mors interitum, et vita accepit principium. ... in qua collata sunt omnia dona gratiarum."[27] Furthermore, the Pontiff added that the same principle (that is, ordination on Sunday) is preserved should the sacrament be conferred on the night of the Ember Saturdays, because the Mass of the vigil is celebrated at the end of the night, at the dawn of Sunday, and thus ordinations fall on the day which commemorates the resurrection of our Saviour.[28] It can be noted that the vigil began at nightfall and ended at dawn on Sunday. The Mass of the vigil took the place of a Sunday Mass.[29]

26 St. Leo, *Epistle IX* [*ad Dioscorum*]: "Quod a patribus nostris praepensiori cura novimus esse servatum, a vobis quoque volumus custodiri, ut non passim diebus omnibus sacerdotalis vel levitica ordinatio celebretur, ... non tantum ex consuetudine, sed etiam ex apostolica novimus venire doctrina, scriptura manifestante, quod, cum apostoli Paulum et Barnabam ex Spiritus sancti praecepto ad evangelium gentibus mitterent praedicandum, jejunantes et orantes imposuerunt eis manus, ut intelligamus, quanta et dantium et accipientium devotione sit curandum, ne tantae benedictionis sacramentum negligenter videatur impletum. Et ideo pie et laudabiliter apostolicis morem gesseris institutis, si hanc ordinandorum formam sacerdotum per ecclesias, quibus Dominus praeesse te voluit etiam ipse servaveris, ut his, qui consecrandi sunt, numquam benedictio, nisi in die dominicae resurrectiones tribuatur, cui a vespere sabbati initium constat ascribi ..." — *MPL*, LIV, 625; Mansi, V, 1241; JK, n. 406; De Puniet, *The Roman Pontifical*, p. 95; cc. 4, 5, D. LXXV.

27 St. Leo, *Epistola ad Dioscorum* — *MPL*, LIV, 625; Mansi, V, 1241; De Puniet, *op. cit.*, p. 96; cc. 4, 5, D. LXXV.

28 St. Leo, *Epist. IX ad Dioscorum*: "...sed post diem sabbati ejusque noctis, quae in prima sabbati lucescit, exordia consecrandi eligantur, in quibus his, qui consecrandi sunt, jejunis et a jejunantibus sacra benedictio conferatur. Quod ejusdem observantiae erit, si omne ipso die dominico, continuato sabbati jejunio, ordinatio celebratur, a quo tempore praecendentis noctis initia non recedunt, quod ad diem resurrectionis (sicut etiam in pascha Domini declaratur) pertinere non dubium est." — *MPL*, LIV, 625; Mansi, V, 1245; c. 4, D. LXXV.

29 De Puniet, *The Roman Pontifical*, p. 95.

Finally, from what has been said, it is obvious that these three sacred orders were given during the sacrifice of the Mass.

The four ember weeks with their fasts were already observed at Rome at the time of Leo, as is evident from his own words. It is not clear, however whether or not ordinations were then assigned to these days.[30] In the brief time which transpired from the death of Leo until the pontificate of Gelasius I (492-496), the ember days became certainly designated as the time for ordination to the priesthood and the diaconate.[31] About the year 494, Gelasius, writing to the Bishops of Luciana, Bruttium (Calabria) and Sicily, in chapter XIII of his epistle stated as follows: "Ordinationes etiam presbyterorum et diaconorum nisi certis temporibus et diebus exercere non debent, idest quarti mensis jejunio, septimi et decimi, sed et etiam quadragesimalis initii, ac mediana quadragesimae die, sabbati jejunio circa vesperam noverint celebrandas."[32] Actually this epistle contained some new and definite rules only for the Sacred Orders of priesthood and diaconate. Quite distinctly the Ember Saturdays are now the days for the conferring of these Orders, as that is what is meant by the expression "jejunio quarti mensis, septimi, et decimi"—that is, the fasts during the months of June, September and December, for the ancient Christians, like the Romans, began their year with March.[33] This is also stated in the *Glossa Ordinaria* to

[30] Thomassinus, *Vetus et Nova Disciplina,* Pars II, Lib. II, Cap. XII, n. 12.

[31] *Loc. cit.*

[32] St. Gelasius I, *Epistola I ad dilectissimos fratres universos episcopos per Lucaniam, et Brutios et Siciliam constitutos, cap. XIII — Bullarum Diplomatum et Privilegiorum Sanctorum Pontificum Taurinensis Editio* (24 vols. et Appendix, Augustae Taurinorum, 1857-1872), I, 104 (hereafter cited *Taurinensis Bullarum Editio;* c. 7, D. LXXV; JK, n. 636; Mansi, VIII, 40; *MPL,* LIX, 52; *Epistolae Romanorum Pontificum Genuinae et Quae ad Eos Scriptae Sunt, a S. Hilaro ad Pelagium II,* Vol. I, *A S. Hilaro Hormisdam.* (edited by Andreas Thiel, Brunsbergae, 1868) I, 360 (hereafter cited Thiel).

Thiel, Mansi and Migne list the quoted passage as chapter XI.

[33] Gasparri (1852-1934), *Tractatus Canonicus de Sacra Ordinatione* (2 vols., Parisiis, 1893), I, n. 57 in footnote (hereafter cited *De Sacra Ordinatione*).

the *Decretum Gratiani*, which explains that the phrase *"quadragesimalis initii jejunio"* refers to the first week of Lent;[34] and that the phrase *"mediana quadragesimae die"* refers to Passion Saturday or *"Sitientes."*[35] It may be noted that the fast or ember week of June (*"quarti mensis"*) was the Saturday of Pentecost week.[36] Gelasius, therefore, limited ordinations to the priesthood and the diaconate to these specific days; all other days were excluded as no longer in accord with ecclesiastical regulations.

Another change brought about by the epistle of the Pontiff was his direction that the ordinations were to be held *"circa vesperam"* of the previously mentioned Saturdays. Gasparri believed that the reason for the change is to be found in the desire to shorten the fast of the ordaining minister and of the ones to be ordained, especially since Sunday begins with the vespers of Saturday, according to the rule of the synagogue, which rule was accepted by the Church.[37]

The so-called *Gelasian Sacramentary* repeated these instructions of the Pope with regard to the days for conferring Sacred Orders, but in a note that preceded the liturgical prayers the subdiaconate was included.[38] This gives rise to some difficulty, for only much later, namely during the pontificate of Alexander III (1159-1181), is there found any positive regulation dealing with the subdiaconate.[39] Hence it might be that this direction is an interpolation. It would seem so from a comparison with the *Sacramentary of Gregory the Great* (590-604). In this book there is mention, in a heading to the order for ordaining, of priests and deacons, but the subdeacon is not put in the same category.[40] Therefore the subdiaconate at that time was still conferred as a minor order.

[34] *Glossa Ordinaria* ad c.7, D. LXXV, s.v. *quadragesimalis.*

[35] *Ibidem,* s.v. *mediana.*

[36] *Ibid.,* s.v. *quarti.*

[37] Gasparri, *De Sacra Ordinatione,* I, n. 57.

[38] *Gelasian Sacramentary,* Lib. I, XX: "Ordo qualit. in Romana sedis apostolicae ecclesia presbyteri, diaconi, vel subdiaconi elegendi sunt." — *MPL,* LXXIV, 1069.

[39] JL, n. 13948; c.3, X, *de temporibus ordinationum et qualitate ordinandorum,* I. 11.

[40] *Gregorian Sacramentary*: "Ordo qualiter in Romana Ecclesia diaconi et presbyteri ordinandi sunt." — *MPL,* LXXVIII, 220.

The *Gregorian Sacramentary* has an interesting remark immediately before giving the prayers for the Minor Orders. For the first time there is some direction with regard to the conferring of Minor Orders, namely, they are to be given after the Communion of the Mass.[41] Although it was neither clear nor definite at what time the Minor Orders might be given, this statement implied that occasionally, at least, they might be given on Sunday. Just what kind of necessity was required for this action was not determined. Furthermore, the statement also showed that the Minor Orders might be given during Mass; but whether or not this was of obligation was not made clear. At least it may be concluded from this statement that the Minor Orders could be given at times on Sunday and during Mass.

In connection with the various sacramentaries, it may here be appropriate to mention another liturgical work, that is, the *Roman Pontifical.* The *Romano-German Pontifical,* which appeared around 950, did little more than repeat the instruction of Pope Gelasius I. This work stated that "ordinations, even of priests and deacons [are to be held] only at certain times . . . .,"[42] and also that they are to be given "mense primo, quarto, septimo et decimo, sabbatorum die in duodecim."[43] The same directions are also found in the *Pontificale Romanae Curiae,* which appeared during the pontificate of Innocent IV (1243-1254).[44] Hence, the Pontifical merely gives evidence of the existing practice of restricting the ordinations of priests and deacons to the Ember Saturdays.

In the centuries following the important epistle of Gelasius,[45] there was, regarding this specific matter no significant writing of any other pope. Thus there was no new regulation, and no important

[41] *Gregorian Sacramentary*: "Majores gradus ante Evangelium, minores vero post Communionem dantur." — *MPL,* LXXVIII, 218.

[42] Andrieu, *Le Pontifical Romain au Moyen Âge,* Tome I, *Le Pontifical Romain du XII Siècle* (in Vol. 86 of Studi e Testi, Vatican City: Vatican Press, 1938), p. 23.

[43] *Ibid.,* pp. 24, 30, 37.

[44] Andrieu, *Le Pontifical Romain au Moyen Âge,* Tom. II, *Le Pontilcal de la Curie Romaine au XIII Siècle* (in Vol. 87 of *Studi e Testi,* Vatican City: Vatican Press, 1940), p. 337.

[45]*Supra,* P. 8.

changes emanated from the Chair of Peter. During this period, however, there is evidence of a number of particular councils, which either repeated what has already been observed, or brought out some new note. Thus, in 692, the Council in Trullo passed the following: "If any one shall in some stage of the priestly order receive ordination contrary to the prescribed times, let him be deposed."[46] Here is the first example of any penalty imposed for the non-observance of the time established for the receiving of Sacred Orders. It is particularly noteworthy that the penalty was inflicted on the one ordained, and consisted in his being deposed from the grade he had attained.

In the next century, under Pope Zacharias (741-752), there met in 744 an important Roman Council. This council in its eleventh chapter reiterated the law that ordinations to the priesthood were to be held "in the first, fourth, seventh and tenth months."[47] This council added no new note, but it did emphasize the previously established regulations.

Other conciliar enactments appeared in but a few particular councils, none of which added any further development relative to the item of time for ordinations. They merely stated in general terms what has already been seen. Thus, the II Council of Chalon-sur-Saône, (813) decreed in general that "the ordination of priests, of deacons, and of the other lower grades was to be performed at the stated times."[48] A council held in the Diocese of Oviedo, in the year

[46] Can. 15 — "... Si quis vero in aliquo ordine sacerdotali praeter constituta tempora ordinatus fuerit, deponatur." — *Sacrosancta Concilia* (17 vols. in 18, ed. Labbeus-Cossartius, Parisiis, 1671-1672), VI, 1149 (hereafter cited *Concilia*); Percival, *The Seven Ecumenical Councils of the Universal Church. Their Canons and Dogmatic Decrees Together with the Canons of All the Local Synods Which Have Received Ecumenical Acceptance* (New York, 1901), pp. 356-357 (hereafter cited *The Seven Ecumenical Councils*); c. 4, D. LXXVII.

[47] Concilium Romanum (744), cap. XI — *Monumenta Germaniae Historica* (*MGH*), Legum, Sectio III (*Concilia*), Tomus II (ed. Fridericus Maassen, Hannoverae, 1895), pp. 17, 32; *Epitome Canonum Conciliorum tum Generalium tum Provincialium ab Apostolis usque ad Annum MDCIX per Alphabeticum Digesta* (2 vols. in 1, ed. J. Ghilardi, O.P., Monteregali, 1870), II, 344 (hereafter cited Ghilardi).

[48] Can. 23 — *MGH*, Legum, Sectio III (*Concilia*), Tom. II, 278; Ghilardi, II, 345.

1050, also treated this matter in general terms. It stated that the sacrament of Holy Orders was to be administered on the "constituted ember days."[49] As a matter of fact, this regulation received mention only incidentally in as much as the fifth canon primarily instructed the Archdeacon with regard to the knowledge expected of the candidates for Orders. Then, in 1095, a particular council at Clermont passed a canon which again repeated the previous legislation—that is, Orders were to be conferred only on the ember days and on the Saturday before Passion Sunday.[50]

In tracing the development of the law with reference to the element of the time for sacred ordination, one can next give consideration to the *Decretum Gratiani* in the twelfth century. Since it was a collection, it is only normal to expect to find contained therein much of the legislation which has already been treated. Thus, as has been noted in the various footnotes, the *Decretum* contains the Epistles of Pseudo-Anacletus,[51] of Pseudo-Zepherinus,[52] of Leo I,[53] of Gelasius I,[54] and also the decree of the Council in Trullo.[55]

There is, however, a pertinent *palea,* canon 6 of Distinction LXXV, which brings new light to the subject. There it was stated that the time and place for the ordination of clerics up to and including the office of subdeacon is a matter of free choice.[56] Although it is not brought out in the *palea*, the choice must have been that of the bishop, the minister of the sacrament, rather than that of the recipient, as it is the superior who arranges matters, and not the subject. Up to that time it more or less followed as a corollary that, if strict regulations were laid down for the diaconate, the priesthood, and the episcopacy, and these alone were mentioned in the decrees, then the other Orders, the minors and the subdiaconate, could be given at any time. It is this conclusion that finds expression in the *palea.*

[49] Can. 5 — Mansi, XIX, 785; Ghilardi, II, 347.
[50] Can. 24 — Ghilardi, II, 347-348.
[51] C. 1, D. LXXV; *Supra,* p. 2.
[52] C. 3, D. LXXV; *Supra,* p. 3-4.
[53] Cc. 4, 5, D. LXXV; *Supra,* pp. 6-7.
[54] C. 7, D. LXXV; *Supra,* pp. 8.
[55] C. 4, D. LXXVII; *Supra,* p. 11.
[56] C. 6, D. LXXV.

Furthermore, the *palea* stated that "deacons and priests are to be ordained only in a public ordination."[57] This seems to indicate a change from the time of Burchard, who had stated that it was not fitting for ordinations to be celebrated under the observation of the "hearers."[58] Rufinus (12th cent.), however, in his commentary on Gratian, observed that Burchard by "hearers" did not mean the faithful, but rather thought of the catechumens and those who were doing penance outside the church.[59] Therefore, about the only change implied in the *palea* was that ordinations could be celebrated before all, even the catechumens and the penitents.

Section B. The Place for Sacred Ordination

The writings of the popes in the first three centuries do not contain any provisions regarding the place where the sacrament of Holy Orders was to be administered. When there is found some reference to the place for ordination, it is not specific, since it does not determine accurately which church within the diocese is to be the scene for the conferral of Orders. The early texts, as will be seen, strongly limit the bishop's jurisdiction in this matter to the confines of his own diocese. Thus, *The Apostolic Canons* in canon thirty-five, with language denoting a definite prohibition, said that a bishop should not "presume to ordain beyond his own limits, in cities and places not subject to him."[60] To add weight to its prohibition the canon continues: "But if he be convicted of doing so without the consent of those persons who have authority over such cities and places, let him be deposed and those also whom he has ordained."[61]

57 "...diaconi vero atque presbyteri numquam, nisi in publica ordinatione." — c. 6, D. **LXXV.**

58 Burchard, *Decretum,* Lib. II, 7 — *MPL,* CXL, 625.

59 Rufinus, ad D. LXXV — ed. Singer, *Die Summa Decretorum des Magister Rufinus* (Paderborn, 1902), pp. 164-165.

60 *Octoginta quinque Regulae, seu Canones Apostolorum* (Parisiis, 1558), p. 34; Zonaras, *In Canones SS. Apostolorum et Sacrorum Conciliorum Commentaria* (Parisiis, 1618), p. 18; Percival, *The Seven Ecumenical Councils,* p. 596.

61 *Loc. cit.*

This canon did, however, point out that the place for ordination was the bishop's own diocese, and that his power extended over all within his territory. But this right was not so exclusive that permission could not be given to an outside bishoop, as the wording of the canon itself indicates.

In 341 the Council of Antioch enacted legislation which restricted a bishop to his own territory. In both canon 13 and canon 22 this Council forbids bishops to go into the territory of another bishop and there to ordain another's subjects, especially to the Orders of the priesthood and the diaconate. This they could do only when the other bishop gave his consent.[62] The Council even insisted that, if without an invitation a bishop attempted to usurp such power, all that he did would prove void and useless.[63] The voidness related to the exercise of the orders received, but not to its reception, that is, the candidate was really ordained, but he was forbidden to exercise the Orders which he had received. Therefore, although these canons were chiefly concerned with the minister of ordination, nevertheless it may be deduced from them that the place for ordination was a bishop's own diocese.

The Council of Sardica (343) had a canon which may be considered to mean that a bishop was restricted to his own territory. Bishop Januarius proposed to the assembled bishops that it be enacted as not permissible for a bishop to go into another diocese, there to seek for himself ministers whom he would then ordain for his own diocese. The assembled bishops agreed.[64] From the wording of the canon one can conclude that it was forbidden both to solicit in another's diocese, and to ordain the candidates in that place. The canon, however, was not altogether clear with regard to the second point, for a bishop could have sent those whom he had gained to his own diocese and then ordained them in his own diocese. This seems more in

[62] Council of Antioch (341), cans. 13, 22 — Mansi, II, 1314, 1318; Burchard, *Decretum*, I, 71, 108 — *MPL*, CXL, 567, 582; Ivo, *Decretum*, V, 178, 210 — *MPL*, CLX, 379, 387; cc. 6, 7, C. IX, q.2; Percival, *The Seven Ecumenical Councils*, p. 115.

[63] Can. 13 — Mansi, II, 1314.

[64] Council of Sardica (343), can. XVIII — Bruns, *Canones Apostolorum et Conciliorum Saeculorum IV, V, VI, VII* (2 vols., Berolini, 1839), I, 103 (hereafter cited Bruns); Percival, *The Seven Ecumenical Councils*, p. 429.

accord with the wording of the canon, and hence, does not so much restrict the bishop to the place for ordination, as it does restrict him to his own subjects.

The I General Council of Constantinople (381) repeated the earlier prohibition: "Bishops are not to go outside their diocese . . . for the purpose of ordaining . . ."[65] Thus the legislation of the first four centuries, especially that of the I General Council of Constantinople (381), stated that the place for ordination was a bishop's own diocese.

In the year 419 there appeared in Northern Africa a collection of canons called *"The Code of Canons of the African Church"*, which in reality was a collection of the canons of earlier councils, and which received the approval of the two hundred and seventeen Fathers who assembled at Carthage. Canon thirteen has some bearing on the subject at hand. Primarily this canon sets forth that a bishop is not to be consecrated without the consent of the Primate of his province, even though many bishops shall be assembled. "But," the canon continues, "should there be a necessity, then at his bidding three bishops shall ordain him in any place they happen to be . . ."[66] Thus, at least for the African Church, the consecration of a bishop seemed to be limited to the province. This, of course, could be representative of the practice in other areas, but, at this early period, no such definite indication existed. So again, as in the previous enactments, the place of ordination was determined only in very wide limits, i.e., any place in the diocese or province seemed to come within the law.

Joseph Bingham (1668-1723), a non-Catholic author who dealt with the antiquities of the Christian Church, has offered some pertinent remarks. He stated that every bishop, by the laws and customs of the Church, was to be ordained in his own church. He concluded this from St. Cyprian (c.200-258) who stated that to celebrate or-

65 Can. 2. "Non vocati autem episcopi ultra dioecesim ne transeant ad ordinationem . . ." — Mansi, III, 559; c. 9, C. IX, q.2; Schroeder, *Disciplinary Decrees of the General Councils: Text, Translation and Commentary* (St. Louis: Herder, 1937, pp. 150-151.

66 *MPL,* LXVII, 188; *Concilia,* II, 1056; Percival, *The Seven Ecumenical Councils,* p. 448.

dinations correctly the neighboring bishops of the province were to meet at the church where the new bishop was to be ordained, and there to proceed to his election and ordination.[67] This seemed to make the place for the ordination of a bishop his own cathedral.

The II Council of Orleans (533) in its seventh canon directed that the metropolitan was to be ordained by all his suffragans,[68] who had gathered together to chose, with the clergy and people, a successor to fill the vacant see. Consequently, the place for the consecration of the metropolitan, as established by Orleans, was the see city of the province and the cathedral, as it would be called today.[69] Hence it may be said that from the earliest times, definitely from the sixth century, it was the practice that the metropolitan should be ordained in his own church in his own diocese. This is the most certain clarification of the place for ordination to be found so far.

This same provision may be found in an apocryhal letter of Pope St. Anicetus (155?-166?), which letter found its way into the collections of canon law.[70]

In 538 the III Council of Orleans treated of the problem of bishops ordaining in another's diocese. Very clearly it stated that "a bishop must not invade another's diocese for the purpose of ordaining another's clerics ..."[71] The regulation itself was not new, but further on a penalty was inflicted on the ordaining minister, namely a suspension from the celebration of Mass for a year.[72] Thus, not

[67] *Epistola XL* — *MPL,* IV, 400; Bingham, *Antiquities of the Christian Church* (reprinted from the original edition of 1708-1722, London, 1856), Bk. II, Chap. XI, Sec. 7.

[68] "Itaque metropolitanus episcopus a comprovincialibus episcopis, clericis vel populis electus, congregatis in unum omnibus conprovincialibus episcopis ordinetur, ..." — *MGH,* Legum Sectio III (*Concilia*), Tome I, 62; Bruns, II, 186.

[69] Bingham, *Antiquities of the Christian Church,* Bk. II, Chap. XVI, Sec. 15.

[70] *Ad Episcopos Galliae,* cap. I — JK, n. 57; Mansi I, 683; Burchard, *Decretum,* I, 28 — *MPL,* CXL, 556; *Hinschius,* p. 120; Ivo, *Decretum,* V, 139 — *MPL,* CLXI, 370; Ivo, *Panormia,* III, 10 — *MPL,* CLXI, 1152; Deusdedit, I, 75 — V. Wolf von Glonvel, *Die Kanonessammlung des Kardinals Deusdedit* (Paderborn, 1905), p. 69; c. 1, D. LXVI; Anselmi *Lucensis' Collectio,* VI, 33 — Thaner, p. 284.

[71] III Council of Orleans, can. XV — Bruns, II, 196.

[72] *Loc. cit.*

only was it enjoined that a transgressor should be punished, but the punishment itself was determined. The same prohibition and penalty in almost identical terms are found in the *Decretum Gratiani,* which cited a letter of Pope Anacletus (76?-88?).[73] Once again it is to be noted that the letter is spurious.[74] But the legislation of the III Council of Orleans (538) reflects the fact that by the sixth century it was the practice to limit to the bishop's own territory his right of conferring Orders.

A few years later Arles was the meeting place for another council which passed rules for the consecration of a bishop. It legislated that a bishop was to be ordained in the city in which he was elected, and in the church over which he was to preside. If for some quickly arising necessity it became impossible to fulfill this enactment, then, although it was preferable that he be ordained in his own church, he could be ordained either in the metropolitan city, or, with the metropolitan's consent, in any place within the province.[75] This provincial council determined in explicit words that the place for the consecration of a bishop (here suffragans) was his own city and his own church.

There was legislation on the subject of the place for ordination in the IV Council of Toledo (633). Its nineteenth canon, after listing impediments to episcopal consecration, continues: "Episcopus autem comprovincialis ibi consecrandus est, ubi metropolitanus elegerit; metropolitanus autem non nisi in civitate metropoli, comprovincialibus ibidem convenientibus."[76] This provincial council enacted very definite rules for its territory. As can be seen, the place for the consecration of a suffragan bishop was left to the choice of the metropolitan, but, as is obvious, it was to be some place within the province. On the other hand, the place for the consecration of the metropolitan was determined more accurately and exclusively—the metropolitan city. This law eventually was incorporated verbatim in the *Decretum Gratiani.*[77]

73 C. 28, C. VII, q.1.
74 JK, n.6.
75 *MGH,* Legum, Sectio III, (*Concilia*), I. 88.
76 IV Council of Toledo, can. 19 — Bruns, I, 229-230.
77 C. 5, D. LI.

In the II General Council of Nicaea (787) there is a relevant canon. The pertinent part of the fourteenth canon reads: "Each *hegumenos* is permitted in his own monastery to ordain a reader, if he himself has been raised to the dignity of *hegumenos* by the laying on of hands by the bishop and is known to be a priest. Similarly, in accordance with an ancient custom, chorepiscopi may ordain readers with the approval of the bishop."[78] The canon treated of the right which the head of a monastery had with regard to granting the Minor Order of the lectorate. The *hegumenos,* if he was a priest and had been raised to this office by the imposition of hands by the bishop (i.e., the abbatial blessing), was restricted in the exercise of his right to his own monastery. Explicitly, the canon mentioned only the Minor Order of the lectorate, but gradually this privilege was extended so that, at least by the I General Council of the Lateran (1123), it included all the Minor Orders.[79] According to the law of this general council the place for the ordination of monks to the order of the lectorate (and gradually for all the Minor Orders) was the monastery, if the ordination was performed by a priest who had been installed in the office of *hegumenos* by the imposition of hands by the bishop. Likewise, a chorepiscopus had the same power, but it was restricted in that he needed the approval of the bishop, who, so it seems, at the time of granting this permission determined also the place. Thus the place for the ordination of a reader by a chorepiscopus was the place properly designated by the bishop. If the latter did not determine the place, then it had to remain within the territory of the bishop, as his jurisdiction extended no farther.

The last important act of legislation, for this period, on the place of ordination is found in the I General Council of the Lateran (1123). In the beginning of the seventeenth canon certain actions were forbidden to abbots and monks; then, the canon continues: "the chrism, holy oil, consecration of altars and ordination of clerics they shall obtain from the bishops in whose dioceses they reside."[80]

[78] II Council Nicaea, can. 14 — Schroeder, *Disciplinary Decrees of the General Councils,* pp. 150-151.

[79] Schroeder, *op. cit.,* p. 190.

[80] I General Council of the Lateran, can. XVII — Mansi, XXI, 285; c.10, C. XVI, q.1.

The identical law was incorporated by Gratian in his ***Decretum*** and came from Pope Calixtus II (1119-1124). Schroeder (1875-1942) assigned as a reason for this prohibition on the part of the Lateran Council the fact that there was an ever increasing encroachment of the monks on parochial ministrations, and much more so in their frequent and flagrant invasion of episcopal rights and privileges. He stated: "That causes of this nature were at the bottom of the present canon can scarcely be doubted."[81] It may be concluded, then, that, although this law of the ecumenical council was chiefly concerned with the minister of the sacrament, still the place for the ordination of monks to Sacred Orders was the diocese in which the monastery was located. Minor Orders could be granted to the monks in their own monastery by the abbot, as was noted above.[82]

In this canon is reflected the historical development of the law regarding the place for ordination as it stood up to the time of Gratian's *Decretum* (ca. 1140). He added nothing new to what has already been mentioned, but simply included in his ***Decretum*** those important acts which have already been indicated. Thus, the *Decretum Gratiani* contains canons 13 and 22 of the Council of Antioch (341);[83] canon 2 of I General Council of Constantinople (381);[84] the apocryphal letter of Anicetus;[85] the spurious epistle of Anacletus;[86] canon 19 of IV Council of Toledo (633);[87] and the decretal letter of Calixtus II (1119-1124).[88]

The further growth of legislation on the time and place of sacred ordination will be taken up in the next chapter.

81 Schroeder, *Disciplinary Decrees of the General Councils,* p. 190.

82 *Supra,* p. 18.

83 *Supra,* p. 14; cc. 6, 7. C. IX, q.2.

84 *Supra,* p. 15; c. 9, C. IX, q.2.

85 *Supra,* p. 16; c. 1, C. LXVI.

86 *Supra,* p. 17; c. 28, C. VII, q. 1.

87 *Supra,* p. 17; c. 5, D. LI.

88 *Supra,* p. 19; c. 10, C. XVI, q. 1.

CHAPTER II

FROM 1150 TO THE COUNCIL OF TRENT

Not long after the *Decretum Gratiani* had made its appearance, Alexander III (1159-1181) issued some decretal letters which have a definite bearing on the topic of time and place for sacred ordination. One of these letters was addressed to the Bishop of Bath in Somersetshire, England, and contained three separate regulations.[1] The first stated that the subdiaconate should not be given on Sunday, except by the Roman Pontiff. Alexander's prohibition made it evident that to ordain a subdeacon on Sunday was a prerogative of the Holy See, which could not be utilized by the other bishops unless they obtained a special permission. This was plainly indicated in the *Glossa Ordinaria*.[2] The second regulation in this particular epistle allowed the conferring of the Minor Orders on Sunday. As soon as the Pope had stated that no one may ordain a subdeacon on Sunday, he added: "quamvis . . . minores ordines his diebus habeant licentiam celebrandi."[3] The final rule in this epistle was another prohibition, which forbade the celebration of Sacred Orders on the Saturday before Pentecost.[4]

The Bishop of Hereford presented two cases to Alexander for solution. The Bishop inquired about the licitness of a custom that was being followed in certain churches in Scotland and Wales. When a church or an altar was dedicated outside the fasts of the ember weeks, clerics were also promoted to Orders. Alexander in disposing of the case called such a custom "inimical to the institution of the Church, detestable, and thoroughly discreditable."[5] He stated that the practice could be allowed to continue only if it was an ancient

[1] C. 1, X, *de temporibus ordinationum et qualitate ordinandorum,* I, 11; JL, n. 13769.

[2] *Glossa Ordinaria* ad c.1, X, *de temp. ordin.*, I, 11, s.v. *Romano.*

[3] C. 1, X, *de temp. ordin.,* I, 11.

[4] *Loc. cit.*

[5] C. 2, X, *de temp. ordin.,* I, 11; JL, n. 13948.

custom of the land. Furthermore, the ones thus ordained ought not to be permitted to exercise the Orders they had received, except in consideration for the ancient custom. In Rome the ones thus ordained (outside the Ember Weeks) would be deposed, and the ones ordaining in that way would be deprived of their authority of ordaining. This reply made it very clear that Sacred Orders were not to be given outside the proper times.

In the second case the Bishop of Hereford wanted to know if it was licit to promote anyone to the four Minor Orders, or even to the subdiaconate, outside the Ember Days. Alexander's response is not an unqualified affirmation. Rather, he stated that it was allowable to advance one or two candidates to Minor Orders on Sundays and feast days (*diebus festivis*), but that no bishop could ordain anyone to the subdiaconate except on the Ember Days, on Holy Saturday, or on the Saturday before Passion Sunday. Only the Roman Pontiff could licitly ordain at other times.[6] Thus ordination to the subdiaconate was placed under the same restrictive regulation as ordination to the diaconate or the priesthood, in as much as the subdiaconate came at that time to be numbered amongst the Sacred or Major Orders.[7] The *Glossa Ordinaria* indicated that more than two, even "several", could be promoted to Minor Orders on a Sunday or a feast day, as long as it did not appear to be a general ordination.[8] Hence the important things in Alexander's response were the reassurance that the Minor Orders could be given on Sundays and festive days outside the regular times, as long as there was not the appearance of a general ordination; and the clarification that the subdiaconate could be conferred only at the times designated for the conferring of the diaconate and the priesthood.

Urban III (1185-1187) in replying to the Archbishop of Pisa added a further note. Again there had been presented a case in which a bishop undertook to confer Orders, while he was dedicating a church on a day not instituted for ordaining. Urban directed that the bishop was to be corrected with canonical discipline, and that the ones thus ordained by him were to be deprived of using their Orders

[6] C. 3, X, *de temp. ordin.*, I, 11; JL, n. 13948.

[7] Gasparri, *De Sacra Ordinatione*, I, n. 35.

[8] *Glossa Ordinaria* ad c. 3, X, *de temp. ordin.*, I, 11, s.v. *aut duos.*

until they had received a dispensatioon from the Holy See.[9] In its explanation the *Glossa Ordinaria* stated that the "canonical discipline" consisted in suspending the bishop from bestowing in the future the Order which he had illicitly conferred. E.g., if he had ordained a subdeacon at a forbidden time, then he could not confer the Order of subdeaconship, though he could confer the other Orders. Also, the offending minister, in the absence of any inflicted penalty, could be punished at the direction of his superior.[10] Furthermore, the granting of a dispensation from the suspension imposed on the ordained was reserved exclusively to the Pope.[11] The fact that a punishment was inflicted for non-conformity with the law definitely strengthened the law regarding the time for sacred ordination, and showed that it was the mind of the legislator to see the law observed inviolably.

In 1199 a particular council in Dalmatia enacted legislation in accord with what has been seen. It stated that the times for ordination were simply the Ember Days, and that only the Roman Pontiff could rightfully ordain a subdeacon on Sunday.[12] This shows that the rules mentioned in the responses of the popes were observed in places other than the dioceses to which their letters had been sent, and thus reflects that their responses were regarded as the equivalents of universal legislation.

A reply was furnished also by Innocent III (1198-1216) in a matter having reference to the time for ordination. He touched on this matter when he wrote to his Cardinal Legate, who wanted help in solving a problem of election in the church of Armagh. The Pope reproved a bishop, because he had ordained someone an acolyte during his own Mass of consecration, and added that this was "permissible only to the Roman Pontiff."[13] The Pope also stated: "Praeterca cum non liceat archiepiscopo sine pallio . . . ordinare clericos, . . . multum profecto praesumit, qui, antequam impetret pallium, clericos

[9] C. 8, X, *de temp. ordin.*, I, 11; JL, n. 15742.

[10] *Glossa Ordinaria* ad c. 8, X, *de temp. ordin.*, I, 11, s.v. *canonica.*

[11] *Ibidem,* s.v. *apud nos.*

[12] Concilium in Dalmatia, c. 2 — Mansi, XXII, 701; Ghilardi, II, 350.

[13] C. 28, X, *de electione et electi potestate,* I, 6; Potthast *Regesta Pontificum Romanorum inde ab Anno Post Christum Natum* 1198 *ad* 1304 (Berolini, 1874-1875), n. 1735 (hereafter cited Potthast).

ordinare festinat . . ."[14] In a sense, these two prescriptions limited the time for ordination to the extent that two definite occasions were excluded, i.e., the bishop's own Mass of consecration, and the interval preceding the archbishop's obtaining of the pallium, even though the Ember Days intervened.

Gasparri stated that there was one case wherein it was licit without a dispensation to confer Major Orders outside the indicated times, that is, if on Saturday on account of the number to be ordained or for some other cause (e.g., sudden sickness of the ordaining bishop) the ordination could not be completed, then on the following Sunday the rest could be ordained, provided the fast was continued. He based this conclusion on a statement of Innocent III.[15]

In the *Glossa* a question was raised whether the Sacred Orders were to be considered as given on Sunday or on Saturday.[16] Huguccio (Hugh of Pisa, d.1210) was of the opinion that all Orders were to be conferred on Sunday, adducing as proof the words of the *Decretum Gratiani,* "post diem sabbati eiusdem noctis, quae lucescit in prima sabbati exordia consecrandi eligantur."[17] In which case those who were to be consecrated were to fast, and the sacred blessing was to be given by one likewise fasting. The observance was to be the same if the ordination was celebrated on Sunday morning upon a continuance of the fast from Saturday. Others, however, held that the Orders which were celebrated on Sunday were to be regarded as attracted to Saturday. Hence the ordination was to be regarded as occurring on Saturday, for Saturday signified rest, and he who became ordained passed to clerical rest—that is, rested from wordly labors.[18] Vincentius (✠ca.1240) stated that this problem centered only around Holy Saturday, since the Mass then was drawn to the following Sunday, and the Orders retracted to Saturday.[19] Innocent IV (1243-1254) in his *Commentaria* observed that at his

[14] *Loc. cit.*

[15] Gasparri, *op. cit.,* I, n. 66; Innocentius IV, *In V Libros Decretalium Commentaria* (Venetiis, 1570), Lib. I. Tit. XI, c. 13 (hereafter cited *Commentaria*).

[16] *Glossa Ordinaria* ad c. 13, X, *de temp. ordin.,* I, 11, s.v. *pertinere.*

[17] C. 4, D. LXXV; *Glossa Ordinaria* ad c. 4, D. LXXV, s.v. *sabbati.*

[18] *Glossa Ordinaria,* ad c. 4, D. LXXV, s.v. *sabbati.*

[19] C. 3, X, *de temp. ordin.,* I, 11.

time ordinations were conferred at night only on Holy Saturday, and not on any other Saturday evening. He, however, accepted the opinion that the Orders were to be considered as conferred on Saturday, and not on Sunday, as Huguccio had thought, "for", so Innocent argued, "if the ordinations are performed on Sunday, why should the fast continue?"[20] The question eventually was solved when Mass began to be celebrated exclusively in the morning, and thus definitely on Saturday.

In 1231, Gregory IX (1227-1241) wrote to the Archbishop of Bari, who wanted to know if one ordained outside the specified times actually received the Order; and, if so, could he be permitted to exercise that Order. Gregory stated clearly that, even though the canonical regulation regarding the time for ordination was not observed, "there was no doubt that they [the candidates] had received the character."[21] The Archbishop was also told that he could allow such an ordained person to exercise his Order, but only after a fit penance had been performed.[22]

The *Glossa Ordinaria* indicated that the character was received, because time is not of the substance of the Order; nevertheless, the one ordained was penalized by being suspended from the exercise of his Order, and the one ordaining was suspended from the function of ordaining. [23] The *Glossa* also inquired whether the power of dispensing the ordained cleric belonged to the bishop, or only to the Roman Pontiff. From the wording it could seem that the bishop might dispense such a one—"quas pro transgressione huiusmodi sustinere poteris in susceptis ordinibus ministrare." But this insinuated a conflict with a previous enactment, in which the pope had reserved to himself the removal of the suspension.[24] It was argued that the power for dispensing was specifically granted in this response of Gregory, whereas in the other response Urban III had set up the

[20] Innocentius IV, *Commentaria,* Lib. I, T. XI, c. 13.

[21] *Les Registres de Grégoire* IX (ed. Lucien Auvray, 3 vols., Paris, 1896-1907), n. 740; Potthast, n. 8832; c. 16, X, *de temp. ordin.,* I, 11.

[22] *Loc. cit.*

[23] *Glossa Ordinaria* ad c. 16, X, *de temp. ordin.,* I, 11, s.v. *characterem.*

[24] C. 8, X, *de temp.* ordin., I, 11 — *supra,* pp. 21-22.

reservation explicity inasmuch as the case was brought to the certain knowledge of the Pope himself.[25]

Once again by the response of Gregory it was shown that the stated times had to be observed, especially with regard to the Major Orders. Hostiensis (d.1271) in his commentary made a good summary of the proper times, namely, the four Ember Saturdays, Passion Saturday, and Holy Saturday for the subdiaconate, the diaconate, and the priesthood; the same four Ember Saturdays, also all Sundays, the festive days for the Minor Orders; and any day whatsoever for first tonsure, since the canons did not expressly call for any certain day, and custom has it so.[26]

Clement IV (1265-1268) was faced with a special problem. Some clerics, who were either excommunicated, or apostates, or irregular, or in some other way unworthy of receiving Orders, had fled their country, in which these facts were known, and sought to be advanced to Orders in remote places, where these facts remained unknown. Clement, desiring to ward off harm to souls, decreed that no bishop of Italy should presume to ordain such a cleric, unless he received special permission from Rome, or from the bishop in whose diocese the candidate had his place of origin or held a benefice, and then only when his own bishop had special reasons for not wishing to ordain the cleric. Clement strengthened this ruling by suspending any bishop who presumed to act contrary to this rule, and he reserved the dispensation to himself, giving little assurance that he would dispense. Further, the one ordained was likewise suspended, and this suspension was likewise reserved.[27] The decree, then, limited the place of ordination in this particular case only in Italy.

[25] *Glossa Ordinaria* ad c. 16, X, *de temp. ordin.*, I, 11, s.v. *poteris.*

[26] Hostinesis (Henricus de Segusio), *In Decretalium Libros Commentaria* (5 vols. in 3, Venetiis, 1581), Lib. I, Tit. XI, c. 16; Panormitanus (1386-1453), *Commentaria in Quinque Libros Decretalium* (5 vols. in 7, Venetiis, 1588), Lib. I. Tit. XI, c. 16.

Both give the verse:

Vult crux, lucia cineres charismata dia
Ut det vota pia, quarta sequens feria.

[27] C. 1, *de temporibus ordinationum et qualitate ordinandorum,* 1, 9, in VI°.

The II General Council of Lyons in 1274 issued a canon on the place of ordination. In its fifteenth canon it decreed "that those who knowingly or through affected ignorance or any other studied fabrication, presume to ordain clerics of another diocese without the permission of the superior of the *ordinandi* are suspended for one year from the conferring of orders; those things that the laws decree against those so ordained are to remain in force. To the clerics of the dioceses of those bishops so suspended, after their suspension has become known, we grant the liberty of receiving sacred orders in the meantime from neighboring bishops who are in good standing, even without the permission of their suspended ordinaries."[28] The Council states implicitly that the place for ordination was the diocese of the candidate's proper bishop. It made this law effective by imposing a one-year suspension from conferring Orders on a bishop if he presumed to ordain outside his proper diocese without the necessary permission. The Council also stated that such ordained clerics were under the penalty of the law, which, as seen before, was suspension from the exercise of the Order received. This canon added a new notion in that it gave permission to clerics, if their bishop was suspended, to be ordained in the meantime by a neighboring bishop, even without the permission of their own suspended ordinary. Hence this made the place for ordination a matter of choice for the clerics, but limited it to a neighboring diocese.

Boniface VIII (1294-1303) stated in a decree that no cleric was to be ordained without the permission of his superior. He further clarified who this superior was, namely, the bishop of the diocese in which the cleric had his origin, or had obtained an ecclesiastical benefice, or had a domicile, even though he had not been born there.[29] This clearly determined the proper diocese, and thus the proper place for ordination. Religious, however, even in exempt monasteries could be licitly ordained in the diocese where the monastery was situated, even though the diocese was not their place of origin.[30]

[28] II General Council of Lyons (1274), c. 15 — Schroeder, *Disciplinary Decrees of the General Councils,* pp. 344, 600; Ghilardi, II, 351; c. 2, *de temporibus etc.,* I, 9, in VI°.

[29] C. 3, *de temporibus, etc.* I, 9, in VI°.

[30] *Loc. cit.*

The decretal law may be summarized thus: regarding the place, it was still the diocese of the candidate's proper bishop. The only change in this regard was the fact that clerics of suspended bishops could seek Orders from a neighboring bishop;[31] regarding time, for the episcopate, it was still any Sunday in the year; for the Major Orders, it was the four Ember Saturdays, Passion Saturday, and Holy Saturday; and for the Minor Orders, it was the same Saturdays, plus any Sunday or festive day, as long as the function was not a general ordination; and for tonsure, it was any day of the year.

31 *Supra,* p. 26.

CHAPTER III

FROM THE COUNCIL OF TRENT (1545-1563) TO THE CODE OF CANON LAW (1918)

The Church's law regarding the time and place for ordination has up to this point been treated without any specific effort to trace separately its growth and development with reference individually to the various Orders. The present chapter will be divided into articles on Tonsure, on the Minor Orders, on the Major Orders, and on the Episcopacy, in order to show more clearly the development of the law and its final form before the publication of the present Code of Canon Law.

Section A. Tonsure

Article 1. The Time for the Conferral of Tonsure

In the period under consideration there was no change in the decretal law with reference to the time for the conferring of tonsure. The *Pontificale Romanum*, indeed, furnished a very concise statement regarding the matter: "First Tonsure may be conferred on any day and at any hour."[1] Thus, the universal law of the Church was

[1] *Pontificale Romanum Summorum Pontificum jussu editum a Benedictio XIV et Leone XIII Pontificibus Maximis Recognitum et Castigatum* (Mechliniae, 1895), Tit. *De Ordinibus Conferendis,* and Tit. *De Clerico Faciendo* (hereafter cited as *Pontificale Romanum*).

The *Pontificale Romanum* was published in 1595. On February 10, 1596, Clement VIII by the Constitution, *Ex quo in Ecclesia Dei,* suppressed all private pontificals and made the *Pontificale Romanum* official and everywhere obligatory. Subsequently, at various intervals, corrections were made of the errors that crept in, and new editions emanated from such Popes as: Urban VIII, in 1644; Benedict XII, in 1725; Benedict XIV, in 1752; Leo XIII, in 1888. None of these typical editions introduced any important changes for the time and place of ordination. Consequently, the edition cited will be accurate for tracing the development of the law. Cf. Catalani. *Commentarium,* Tom I, 115, 132. This work contains the text of Urban VIII, which, for the matter on the time and place of ordination, has been, by comparison, found to be identical with the *Pontificale Romanum* of 1895. Originally, the work of Catalani was published in 1738.

distinctly and permanently established in the matter regarding the time for the conferring of tonsure.

ARTICLE 2. THE PLACE FOR THE CONFERRAL OF TONSURE

The indication of the place for the conferring of tonsure also remained what it had been in the decretal law. The *Pontificale Romanum* repeated the rule in its statement: "First Tonsure may be conferred . . . in any place."[2] "In any place" was to be understood as any place within the diocese. Hence it was not necessary that tonsure be administered in the cathedral church, or in any other specific church; it could be done in the bishop's house, or also elsewhere, even though the place was one not set aside exclusively for divine worship, so long as the place proved decent and respectable.[3]

The question arose quite naturally: Could a bishop confer tonsure in another diocese without the express permission of the local ordinary? It was with reference to this problem that the Council of Trent (1545-1563) enacted the following: "No bishop is allowed under pretext of any privilege to exercise pontifical functions in the diocese of another, except with the expressed permission of the ordinary of the place, and for those persons only who are subject to the same ordinary. If the contrary is done, the bishop is *ipso iure* suspended from the exercise of pontifical functions and those so ordained from the exercise of their orders."[4] At first glance it could seem that the Council categorically and under canonical penalties forbade the conferring of tonsure in another's diocese without an express permission, but actually it merely raised a further difficulty. Was the conferring of tonsure included in the phrase "to exercise pontifical functions" (*pontificalia exercere*)? The solution of the question depended on the meaning of *pontificalia.* According to the common

[2] *Pontificale Romanum,* Tit. *De Ordinibus Conferendis,* and Tit. *De Clerico Faciendo;* Catalani, *Commentarium,* Tom. I, 115, 132.

[3] Gasparri, *De Sacra Ordinatione,* I, n. 91; Schmalzgrueber (1633-1735), *Ius Ecclesiasticum Universum* (5 vols. in 12, Romae, 1843-1845), Lib. I, tit. XI, n. 17 (hereafter cited Schmalzgrueber); Pirhing (1606-1679), *Ius Canonicum in V Libros Decretalium* (5 vols. in 4, Dilingae, 1674-1678), Lib. I, tit. XI, n. 76 (hereafter cited Pirhing).

[4] Sess. VI, *de ref.,* c. 5 — Schroeder, *Canons and Decrees of the Council of Trent, Original Text with English Translation* (St. Louis: B. Herder, 1941), pp. 50, 327.

opinion *pontificalia exercere* signified the performance of episcopal functions when the bishop was vested with the pontifical insignia, i.e., the mitre and the crozier.[5] Thus if the bishop, when vested in the pontificals, wanted to confer tonsure upon a person in another's diocese, he needed the express permission of the local ordinary. This permission, on the other hand, was not required if the bishop without pontificals desired to confer tonsure privately on his own subjects in another's diocese.[6]

Furthermore, in accordance with the decree of the Council of Trent mentioned above, could the bishop in pontificals confer tonsure only on the subjects of the ordinary who granted the permission, so that there were excluded candidates from other dioceses, even when they could present the proper dismissorial letters? The Sacred Congregation of the Council, in 1573, was confronted with a case involving this query. The Archbishop of Naples requested the Bishop of Bisignano to confer tonsure in Naples upon the candidates for Naples, and also upon the candidates for other dioceses. The Congregation replied that this procedure was not forbidden by the decree of the Council of Trent, and accordingly it could be followed.[7] Thus the local ordinary could grant the permission to an outside bishop to tonsure all the candidates, even though they were not his subjects.

Regarding the place for the conferring of tonsure the law before the Code allowed the administration of it in any place within the diocese, and even outside the limits of the diocese if the bishop was not vested with the pontificals and tonsured only his own subjects.

Section B. The Minor Orders

Article 1. The Time for the Conferral of the Minor Orders

The *Pontificale Romanum* directed that "the four minor orders may be given outside of Mass, on Sundays and festive days of double

[5] Gasparri, *De Sacra Ordinatione,* I, n. 96.

[6] Catalani, *Commentarium,* Tom. I, 116.

[7] S.C.C., *Bisinianen.,* 1573 — *Codicis Iuris Canonicis Fontes* cura Emi. Petri Card. Gasparri editi (9 vols., Romae [postea Civitate Vaticana]: Typis Polyglottis Vaticanis, 1923-1939; Vols. VII-IX ed. cura et studio Emi Iustiniani Card. Serédi), n. 2119 (hereafter cited *Fontes*).

rank, but in the morning only."[8] This statement, however, did not exclude the Ember Saturdays, Passion Saturday, or Holy Saturday; rather it indicated, as did the previous decretal law, that the time for the conferring of the Minor Orders could be linked also with other days. There was the added restriction, though, that the administration of these Orders be undertaken only in the morning, even should they be given apart from Mass.

There naturally arose a need of interpretation with reference to the phrase "*festivis diebus duplicibus*". These days were not to be identified with the days which the Church in its office celebrated *sub ritu duplici;* rather, they were days which were observed as holy days by the people, at least in some region, or which were observed as holy days in antiquity, but later had been suppressed by apostolic authority, or in which in their festive celebration had been transferred to another day.[9] Or, to state it another way, as Catalani had earlier done, the festive day in question was one which the clergy and people celebrated as of precept, and on which they rested from servile works, for . . . in the common estimation . . . it was in this manner that the phrase "*dies festus*" was understood.[10] This sense was clarified by the text of the *Pontificale Romanum* of 1895, which added the phrase *ex praecepto,* and accordingly pointed simply to days of precept.[11]

Some questions on this matter were presented to the Sacred Congragation of Rites. In one the Bishop of Marsi asked: "If there has been given to the bishop the faculty of conferring Sacred Orders on feast days, may he confer them on the feasts of the Apostles, and on other feast days abrogated by the Apostolic See? On these same days, however, may he also confer Minor Orders?" On November 12, 1831, the Congragation replied in the affirmative to both parts, but added "in the morning only" for Minor Orders.[12]

8 Tit., *De Minoribus Ordinibus;* Catalani, *Commentarium,* Tom. I, 152.

9 Gasparri, *De Sacra Ordinatione,* I, n. 52.

10 *Commentarium,* Tom. I, 115.

11 Tit. *De Ordinibus Conferendis.*

12 S.R.C., *Marsorum,* 12 nov. 1831, ad 1 — *Decreta Authentica Congregationis Sacrorum Rituum* (5 vols. et 2 appendices, Romae: Ex Typographia Polyglotta, 1898-1927), n. 2682 (hereafter cited *Decr. Auth.*); *Fontes,* n. 5858.

In 1833, a similar request for interpretation was presented to the same Congregation. It replied: "The Minor Orders can be conferred on feasts of precept, or on feasts of double rite which before their reduction were of precept."[13] A few years later, in 1843, the Bishop of Le Puy-en-Velay asked specifically about the Feast of St. John, Apostle and Evangelist, which then was no longer of precept in France. The Sacred Congregation of Rites merely referred the Bishop to the response given to the Bishop of Marsi on November 12, 1831, and so indicated that Minor Orders could be given on this particular day.[14]

Catalani had earlier pointed out that there could be followed, wherever it existed, the custom of conferring Minor Orders on feast days of double rite, even when these days were no longer observed as fo precept by the peoyle.[15] Further, he had also stated that a bishop could safely follow the custom of conferring Minor Orders on the Friday evening which preceded the usual Saturdays of general ordination.[16] The Sacred Congregation of the Council, when questioned about this custom, said that it was lawful to follow it if the custom was immemorial, but that the continuance of such a custom was tolerated, and that the bishop should try to comply with the *Pontificale Romanum,* Tit. *De Minoribus Ordinibus.*[17] Barbosa had taught that a bishop could follow the established custom of his diocese in the pursuance of which Minor Orders were conferred on the Wednesday of an Ember week.[18]

[13] S.R.C., *Claramonten.,* 16 mart. 1833 — *Decr. Auth.,* n. 2705; *Fontes,* n. 5867.

[14] S.R.C.,*Anicien.,* 18 febr. 1843 — *Decr. Auth.,* n. 2852; *Fontes,* n. 5915.

[15] *Commentarium,* Tom. I, 116 § IV.

[16] *Ibidem,* p. 116 § V; Pirhing, Lib. I, tit. XI, n. 78, note 4; Fagnanus (d. 1678), *Commentaria in Quinque Libros Decretalium* (5 vols., in 3, Venetiis, 1697), Lib. I, tit. XI, c. III, n. 42 (hereafter cited Fagnanus); Barbosa (1589-1649), *De Officio et Potestate Episcopi* (2 vols., Lugduni, 1656), P. II, alleg. 10, n. 21.

[17] S.C.C., *Portalegren.,* 13 apr. 1720 — *Thesaurus Resolutionum Sacrae Congregationis Concilii* (167 vols., Urbini-Romae, 1718-1908), I, 285 (hereafter cited *Thesaurus*).

[18] Barbosa, *De Officio et Potestate Episcopi,* P. II, alleg. 10, n. 21.

According to the foregoing, aside from custom, the law of this period concerning the time for the conferring of Minor Orders was the following: they could be conferred on the Ember Saturdays; on Passion Saturday; on Holy Saturday; on all Sundays; and on feasts of precept; on days which were formerly feasts of precept; on feasts of precept which had been transferred to another day by apostolic authority. In addition, these Orders could be conferred only in the morning.

Article 2. The Place for the Conferral of the Minor Orders

The Council of Trent, as mentioned above,[19] stated that no bishop could rightfully exercise pontifical functions in another diocese without the permission of the local ordinary.[20] As was explained previously, this law restricted the bishop to his own diocese whenever he functioned while vested with the pontificals. Therefore the place for the conferring of Minor Orders, when done as a pontifical function, was limited to the confines of the ordaining bishop's diocese. The same conclusion can also be gathered from the second chapter of the fourteenth session of the Council of Trent. Although this particular chapter was concerned primarily with dismissorial letters, incidentally it stated that a bishop could not perform pontifical functions in another's diocese without permission.[21]

In still a later session, the twenty-third, the Council of Trent again, in an incidental way, mentioned the place for the ordination to Minor Orders. The regulation allowed abbots to confer tonsure and Minor Orders only upon their own religious subjects, to the exclusion completely of the secular clergy. "The ordination of all these persons (the seculars) . . . shall pertain to the bishops within the limits of whose diocese they are . . ."[22] In other words, the Council insisted that the place for the ordination to Minor Orders of the secular clergy was the diocese of the candidates.

19 *Supra*, p. 29.

20 Sess. VI, *de ref.*, c. 5 — Schroeder, *Canons and Decrees of the Council of Trent*, pp. 50, 327.

21 Ses. XIV, *de ref.*, c. 2 — Schroeder, *op. cit.*, pp. 107, 381.

22 Sess. XXIII, *de ref.*, c. 10 — Schroeder, *op. cit.*, pp. 170-171, 442.

The *Pontificale Romanum* contained the direction, "minor orders may be given . . . everywhere."[23] By this was meant, as for the administering of tonsure, that the Minor Orders could be conferred in any place within the diocese, and not just in the cathedral or in some other specific church. This direction called for the same interpretation which applied to the conferring of tonsure.[24] Thus the bishop could ordain his subjects to Minor Orders even oustide his own diocese and without the local ordinary's permission, provided he did not wear the pontifical insignia.

Shortly after the Council of Trent, the Archbishop of Lima presented a problem to the Sacred Congregation of the Council. He wanted to know whether any bishop of another diocese could ordain in a monastery of Regulars without the invitation of the proper bishop of the diocese in which the monastery was situated, even though the said monastery had an indult from the Holy See whereby in it ordinations could be celebrated. The Congregation, in February, 1586, replied that this could not be done.[25] In effect, this reply meant that the place for the ordination of Regulars was the diocese within which their monastery was located, and that the ordination pertained to the bishop of that place.

The S. Congregation of Rites, under date of March 30, 1675, sent a decree to the Archbishop of Naples, and declared that it was not permissible that orders be conferred by many bishops, in the same church, at the same time.[26] Even though this declaration was not primarily concerned with the place for the conferring of the Minor Orders, still it indicated that, while the church was being used for ordination, it automatically became restricted, so that it could no

[23] Tit. *De Ordinibus Conferendis;* Catalani, *Commentarium,* Tom. I, 115.

[24] *Supra,* pp. 29-30.

[25] S.C.C., *Civitatis Regalis in Indiis* (*Limana*), mense febr. 1586 — *Fontes,* n. 2152; Pallottini, *Collectio omnium conclusionum et resolutionum quae in causis propositis apud Sacram Congregationem Cardinalium S. Concilii Tridentini Interpretum prodierunt ab eius institutione anno MDLXIV ad annum MDCCCLX, distinctis titulis alphabetico ordine per materias digesta* (17 vols., Romae, 1868-1893), XVI, 153, n. 25 (hereafter cited Pallottini).

[26] S.R.C., *Neapolitana,* 30 mart. 1675 — *Decr. Auth.,* n. 1534.

longer serve as a proper place for any other bishop to confer orders.

The same Congregation was asked by the Bishop of Mazara del Vallo, in Sicily, whether a bishop, if he has the faculty of saying a Mass before the conventual Mass on Holy Saturday, and wants to confer Orders on Holy Saturday, could do so privately in his own chapel or some other place. The reply handed down on March 18, 1702, was: "In the negative."[27] Therefore, on this particular day at least the place of ordination had to coincide with the place where the principal Mass was to be said. The decision, however, was later reversed, when the Bishop of Cebù (Philippine Islands) asked: "Licitne celebrare Missam et Ordines conferre in Sabbato Sancto in Oratorio Episcopali, ante quam celebretur Missa Parochialis?" The reply on May 9, 1857, was: "In the affirmative."[28] The Congregation also referred to its reply of March 24, 1744, as given to the Bishop of Bergamo. This decree stated that the bishop was obliged to celebrate the Mass with the Prophecies, if on Holy Saturday he was to confer Sacred Orders in his domestic oratory.[29] Even though there was express reference to "Sacred Orders", still it was demonstrated that the place for the conferring of Orders included the bishop's private oratory on Holy Saturday. In other words, these decrees eventually interpreted the law as it had been set out in the *Pontificale Romanum,* that is, that Minor Orders could be given "everywhere."

Thus the law regarding the place for the conferring of Minor Orders during this period was the following: They could be given anywhere within the diocese, and even outside the diocese, if without the use of pontificals the bishop ordained his own subjects.

SECTION C. THE MAJOR ORDERS

ARTICLE 1. THE TIME FOR THE CONFERRAL OF THE MAJOR ORDERS

"Ordinationes sacrorum ordinum statutis a jure temporibus . . . celebrentur" is the legislation passed by the Council of Trent on the

27 S.R.C., *Mazarien.,* 18 mart. 1702 — *Decr. Auth.,* n. 2095.

28 S.R.C., *Nominis Jesu,* 9 maii 1857 — *Decr. Auth.,* n. 3044.

29 S.R.C., *Bergomen.,* 24 mart. 1744 — *Decr. Auth.,* n. 2095.

subject of the time for the conferral of Sacred Orders.[30] Thus the Council introduced no change in the existing law, but merely added its own authority to it. The decretal law remained unchanged. It was concisely stated in the *Pontificale Romanum*: "Tempora ordinationum sunt: Sabbata in omnibus quatuor temporibus, Sabbatum ante Dominicam de Passione et Sabbatum Sanctum."[31] Just as the Minor Orders were not given except in the morning, so too the Major Orders, but in addition the later were given only during Mass.[32]

Although there was no further positive legislation on the topic under consideration, still a number of responses emanated from various Roman Congregations. So, in order to end a dispute which had arisen among his masters of ceremonies, the Bishop of St.-Brieuc asked the Sacred Congregation of the Council whether *diebus festis duplicibus, non tamen de praecepto,* Sacred Orders could be conferred on those who have an Apostolic dispensation from the observance of the interstices, or an Apostolic dispensation for the reception of Orders outside the appointed times. On January 15, 1689, the answer came from the Congregation: "In the negative, but only on the feast days of precept."[33] Hence, even when the Holy See granted a dispensation from the observance of the times as stated in the law, it still insisted on the use of days that were of greater liturgical importance than feasts of merely double rite.

To show the strictness of the law regarding the set times for ordination to Sacred Orders, one may point to a reply of the Sacred Congregation of Rites. The Bishop of Segorbe, sixty-two years of age and of feeble health, requested the faculty of transferring the ordination to the priesthood, even though of a small group, to the Sunday immediately after the proper time. The Sacred Congregation on July 4, 1705, refused the permission.[34] It is clear, then, how rigidly these laws called for a complete observance.

30 Sess. XXIII, *de ref.*, c. 8 — Schroeder, *Canons and Decrees of the Council of Trent,* pp. 169, 441.

31 Tit. *De Ordinibus Conferendis;* Catalani, *Commentarium,* Tom. I, 110.

32 Benediltus XIV, *Opera Omnia in Unum Corpus Collecta,* Tom. Undecimus, *De Synodo Dioecesana* (Venetiis, 1788), Lib. VIII, XI, n. 3.

33 S.C.C., *Briocen.,* 15 ian. 1689 — *Fontes,* n. 2908.

34 S.R.C., *Segobricen.,* 4 iul. 1705 — *Decr. Auth.,* n. 2158.

Some time later the Holy Office was asked by a Bishop in Ireland, since he felt pressed with the stress of time, whether he could confer all the Sacred Orders on a Sunday and two feasts of double rite occurring in the same or the following week, when the conferral of the Sacred Orders in this manner could be accomplished without danger and with a greater degree of security. In its reply of March 5, 1712, the Congregation answered: "In the affirmative, on three feasts of precept, not continuous but separated."[35] Again, although some relaxation of the law was granted, yet the conferring of the Sacred Orders was restricted to important liturgical days.

Also on this question, the Administrator of the Archdiocese of Quebec presented a doubt for solution to the Sacred Congregation of Rites. He explained that in the Archdiocese of Quebec, by special indult, the solemnity of certain feasts of precept was transferred to the following Sunday, or, if that Sunday was impeded, then to the preceding Sunday. He inquired whether to a day, when is celebrated the transferred Office or transferred solemnity, there is also transferred the faculty which was given to a bishop of conferring Sacred Orders on feasts of precept. The Congregation on March 6, 1896, replied that the faculty may also be used on the day to which the feast day had been transferred.[36] Thus, when a day of precept was transferred to a Sunday, the ordination to Sacred Orders could also be transferred to the same day, if the bishop had the faculty of conferring these Orders on feast days of precept.

A bishop may have received the faculty of conferring Sacred Orders on feast days, and these days were to be understood as feast days of precept, or feast days which were formerly of precept but were later abrogated by the Holy See. This was explained before when speaking of the minor orders.[37] This same conclusion is derivable from the replies of the Sacred Congregation of Rites to the

[35] S.C.S. Off., 5 mart. 1712 — *Fontes*, n. 776; *Collectanea S. Congregationis De Propaganda Fide* (2 vols., Romae: Ex typographica Polyglotta, S.C. de Propaganda Fide, 1907), I, n. 280 (hereafter cited *Collectanea*).

[36] S.R.C., *Quebecen.*, 6 mart. 1896 — *Decr. Auth.*, n. 3890; *Fontes*, n. 6255.

[37] *Supra*, pp.31-32.

Bishop of Marsi, and to the Bishop of Le Puy-en-Velay, which replies have received previous mention.[38]

From what has been said it is obvious that dispensations from the law could be granted. It may here serve a useful purpose to mention something about the reasons for obtaining such a dispensation. Innocent XII, on December 14, 1693, approved the Instruction of a Special Congregation, which set forth the conditions and the causes that could warrant the granting of a dispensation. This Congregation was especially deputed by the Pope to handle indults for ordinations *extra tempora.* In its Instruction, approved by Innocent, the following were stated:

> "Congregatio censuit indulta hujusmodi [i.e., for ordinations to Sacred Orders *extra tempora*], si SSmo placuerit, concedi posse ex causis infrascriptis, videlicet: Ut quis beneficio, vi cujus arctatur ad presbyteralem ordinem suscipiendum, vel alteri etiam perpetuo beneficio, quod obtinuit, vel cappellaniae ad vitam sibi concessae, per se ipsum inservire possit. Ob penuriam sacerdotum in illis partibus, vel in monasterio pro regularibus. Ob solatium patris vel matris, dummodo quinquagesimum aetatis annum excedant, et Orator saltem per triennium in clericali habitu honeste et laudabiliter vixerit. Item concedi posse censuit eadem indulta referendariis utriusque Signaturae, familiaribus Summi Pontificis, canonicis cathedralis, vel etiam collegiatae ecclesiae eorumque coadjutoribus, magistris, sed etiam baccalaureis in sacra theologia, doctoribus utriusque vel saltem canonici juris, seu licentiatis, dummodo singulos praefatos gradus in publica et approbata universitate obtinuerint. His etiam qui saltem per triennium sedulam theologiae studiis operam navaverint, ac tandem vigesimum sextum aetatis annum excedentibus, si per trienium in clericali habitu

[38] *Supra,* pp. 31-32.

honeste et laudabiliter vixerint."[39]

In this manner were enumerated the causes, and also the conditions according to which a dispensation could be granted. It was also pointed out that the indult was never given for use on consecutive days, but only after some interval, which was to be determined at the discretion of the bishop.[40] Finally, it is important to note that even though the bishop did hold such an indult, he could not be constrained to use it.[41]

Furthermore, when someone was ordained *extra tempora* in virtue of a dispensation granted by the Apostolic See in a particular case, then the apostolic mandate needed to be read before the bishop proceeded to the conferring of Orders. This was the direction of the *Pontificale Romanum*.[42]

Gasparri listed two occasions when Sacred Orders could be conferred outside the proper times without a dispensation, namely: first, if some one was elected as Roman Pontiff, and he was still without these Orders; second, if on a Saturday, on account of the number to be ordained or for some other cause (e.g., sudden sickness of the ordaining bishop), the ordination could not be completed, then on the following Sunday the rest could be ordained. He added that perhaps it could also happen when everything was prepared for the ordination, and the bishop could not begin it for some reason (e.g., sickness). Inasmuch as it would have proved a grave inconvenience, the ordination could be held outside the stated time.[43]

In the course of time problems arose concerning the validity of someone's ordination because of some defect in either the matter or

39 *Magnum Bullarium Romanum* (19 vols. in 18, Luxenburgi, 1727-1754), VII, 294 (hereafter cited *Magnum Bull. Rom.*); Giraldi (1692-1775). *Expostitio Juris Pontificii iuxta recentionem Ecclesiae disciplinam in duas partes distributa* (3 vols. in 2, Romae, 1769) Pars II, sect. 95; Gasparri, *De Sacra Ordinatione,* I, n. 71.

40 *Loc. cit.;* Gasparri, *op. cit.,* I, n. 72.

41 *Loc. cit.*

42 Tit. *De Ordinibus Conferendis;* Catalani, *Commentarium,* Tom. I, 120.

43 *De Sacra Ordinatione,* I, n. 67; Schmalzgrueber, Lib. I, Tit. XI, n. 16; Reiffenstuel (1642-1703), *Jus Canonicum Universum* (5 vols. in 7, Parisiis, 1864-1870), Lib. I, Tit. XI, n. 36; *supra,* p. 41.

the form of the sacrament. If it was an essential defect, the ordination was invalid, and consequently had to be repeated absolultely. Or, at times, when there was some doubt, the repetition had to be undertaken conditionally. Questions were presented to various Congregations regarding the time when such ordinations were to take place. The Sacred Congregation of Rites, on June 16, 1837, and on May 22, 1841, ruled that for defective ordinations the remedy could be sought *opportuno tempora,* or *quacumque anni die.*[44] Therefore the supplying for some defect of ordination could be undertaken any day within the year.

The same direction was given on numerous occasions by the Holy Office, which received the majority of inquires regarding the validity of various ordinations. Thus this Congregation gave such directions as:—*etiam extra tempora generalis ordinationis; quocumque anni tempore; quovis anni tempore.*[45] Therefore the supplying of a ceremony, or the repetition of an ordination to Sacred Orders, when done absolutely or conditionally, could take place on any day in the year.

Although previously any one who ordained outside the proper times, and also the one so ordained, incurred a suspension, this *latae sententiae* penalty was revoked by Clement VIII.[46] And there was no such penalty enacted by the Council of Trent.[47]

In summary, then, the law regarding the time for the conferring of Major Orders, apart of course from any privilege or indult, may be stated as follows: Sacred Orders could be conferred on the Ember Saturdays, on Passion Saturday, and on Holy Saturday. The repeti-

[44] S.R.C., *Taurinen.,* 16 iun. 1837 — *Decr. Auth.,* n. 2767; *Fontes,* n. 5890; *Vivarien.,* 22 maii 1841 — *Decr. Auth.,* n. 2836; *Fontes,* n. 5913.

[45] S.C.S.Off. (Cochinchin.), 19 aug. 1851 — *Collectanea,* I, n. 1066; *Fontes,* n. 917; *Acta Sanctae Sedis* (41 vols., Romae, 1865-1908), XXV (1892) 579-580 (hereafter cited *ASS*); 20 ian. 1875 — *Collectanea,* II, n. 1431; *Fontes,* n. 1038; *ASS,* XXIX (1896), 562-563; (Angliae), 7 sept. 1892 — *Collectanea,* II, n. 1811; *Fontes,* n. 1160; 9 dec. 1897 — *Collectanea,* II, n. 1987; *Fontes,* n. 1194; *Decr. Auth.,* n. 2836. There are many more decisions of a like nature from the Holy Office, but these will serve to exemplify the point.

[46] Const. *Romanum Pontificem,* 28 febr. 1596 — *Fontes,* n. 182.

[47] Gasparri, *De Sacra Ordinatione,* I, n. 81.

tion of an ordination to Sacred Orders, whether absolute or conditional, could be undertaken on any day within the year.

ARTICLE 2. THE PLACE FOR THE CONFERRAL OF THE MAJOR ORDERS

In the decretal law the place for the conferral of Sacred Orders was restricted to the bishop's own diocese. This general rule was also stated in the Council of Trent, when it ruled that no bishop was allowed to exercise pontifical functions in the diocese of another without the permission of the ordinary of the place.[48] Since the Major Orders could not be conferred unless the bishop was vested in pontificals, this decree thereby limited the place for the conferring of Major Orders to the bishop's own diocese.

The Council of Trent added some more details when it decreed: "Ordinationes sacrorum ordinum . . . in cathedrali ecclesia, vocatis praesentibusque ad id ecclesiae canonicis, publice celebrentur; si autem in alio dioecesis loco, praesente clero loci, dignior, quantum fieri poterit, ecclesia semper adeatur."[49] Thus the cathedral church was definitely established as the proper place for the conferring of the Major Orders. It is to be noted, though, that the Council treated of the general ordinations, and so did not forbid the holding of a particular ordination in another place.[50] In the decree just quoted the Council of Trent also directed that the ordination was to be held in public, that is, in the presence of the people and especially of the canons of the cathedral. Even if the ordination was performed in some other church which was to be the more important (*dignior*) church of the locality, at least the local clergy was to be present.

The regulation of the Council of Trent was soon after repeated by provincial and particular councils. As examples, there are the IV Council of Milan in 1576, and the Council of Rouen in 1581.[51]

48 Sess., VI, *de ref.*, c. 5 — Schroeder, *Canons and Decrees of the Council of Trent,* pp. 50, 327; Gasparri, *op. cit.*, I, n. 99.

49 Sess. XXIII, *de ref.*, c. 8 — Schroeder, *op. cit.*, pp. 169, 441.

50 Fagnanus, Lib. V, tit. 3, c. 1, n. 45; Gasparri, *De Sacra Ordinatione,* I, n. 100.

51 Mansi, XXXIV, 233, 633.

It was not very long, however, before difficulties in the interpretation of the decree arose. In 1586 a dispute between the Bishop of Siguenza and his cathedral chapter reached the Sacred Congregation of the Council for solution. The Bishop wanted to hold a general ordination, not in his cathedral, but in a monastery of nuns, which was not far from his residence; moreover, he commanded the chapter to be present under pain of a *latae sententiae* excommunication. It was also the immemorial custom of the diocese that the chapter did not assist the bishop outside the cathedral, unless they accompanied him to the place in procession. The chapter refused to go to the monastery, and was nominally excommunicated by the bishop. The Congregation, then, was asked whether the Bishop was bound to celebrate general ordinations at stated times in the cathedral church; whether he was free to do so in some other church in the see city; and whether the chapter was bound by the decree of the Council of Trent to assist at ordinations outside the cathedral, or whether the immemorial custom held sway. In its answer the Congregation indicated that both had acted wrongly: the Bishop, in that he failed to observe the Tridentine decree, and without an urgent reason ordained outside his cathedral; and the chapter, in that they refused assistance to their Bishop . So the Bishop was directed to absolve the excommunication, and was admonished to celebrate ordinations in his cathedral, unless there was some urgent necessity to do otherwise.[52] Thus the rule of the Council of Trent was enforced, and it was further shown that an urgent necessity was required before a Bishop could ordain to Major Orders in another church in his see city.

A few years later, the canons of the diocese of Gerona complained to the Congregation of the Council that their Bishop was acting against the customs of their church, and was causing harm and scandal. Among the things listed was the fact that the Bishop held general ordinations in a chapel of his palace, or sometimes in the cathedral, but in a remote and obscure chapel, and without calling the canons. The Congregation merely recalled the decree of the Council of Trent that the ordination to Sacred Orders had to be

[52] S.C.C., *Seguntina,* mense iun. 1586 — *Fontes,* n. 2158; Pallottini, XVI, 153, n. 23.

held in the cathedral church, publicly, and in the presence of the canons.[53] On the other hand, the same Congregation, on November 20, 1592, in a response to the Diocese of Mileto stated that, "Si non fuerit ordinatio generalis, sed tantum aliquot paucarum personarum, posse utique Episcopum eam habere etiam in capella sua privata."[54] These responses bear out the interpretation that the Council of Trent directed that the general ordinations be held publicly and in the cathedral church.

The *Pontificale Romanum* incorporated and repeated in its rubrics the enactment of the Council of Trent. It added no further regulation to the law.[55]

In time, however, this decree of the Council was so tempered by custom, that, although commonly the general ordinations were to be held in the cathedral church, nevertheless the bishop could for a reasonable cause select another church.[56] In fact, Hallier (1595-1659) taught that sometimes it was even expedient that the bishop go to another church, especially if the diocese was large. In this way the *ordinandi* would be relieved of making a long journey, and also the people, when they lived at a great distance from the episcopal city, might be inspired to show greater respect to the clergy in view of the solemnity of the ordination which they could witness.[57]

Regarding the place for the conferral of Orders, the Bishop of Mazara del Vallo (in Sicily) asked the Sacred Congregation of Rites whether a bishop, when he had the faculty of saying a Mass before the conventual Mass on Holy Saturday, and wanted to confer Orders on that day, could do so privately in his own chapel or in some other

53 S.C.C., *Gerunden.*, mense mart. 1588; mense aug. 1588 — *Fontes*, nn. 2198, 2202; Pallottini, XVI, 153, n. 19.

54 S.C.C., *Mileten.*, 20 nov. 1592, ad 3, *Fontes*, n. 2252; Pallottini, XVI, 153, n. 21.

55 Tit. *De Ordinibus Conferendis;* Catalani, *Commentarium*, Tom. I, 126.

56 Schmalzgrueber, Lib. I, Tit. XI, n. 17; St. Alphonsus Liguori (1696-1787), *Theologia Moralia* (ed. nova, cura Gaudé, 7 libri in 4 vols., Romae, 1905-1912), Lib. VI, Tract. V, c. 2, dub. 2, n. 798 (hereafter cited Alphonsus).

57 *De Sacris Electionibus et Ordinationibus ex antiquo et novo Ecclesiae Usu* (3 vols., Romae, 1740, Pars III, Sect. VI, art. 1, n. 4 (hereafter cited Hallier).

place. Although the Congregation replied negatively in 1702,[58] nevertheless, as was noted before, it reversed itself later and permitted the bishop's oratory as a place for ordination on Holy Saturday. This permission is known from the replies that were sent to the Bishop of Bergamo in 1744,[59] and the Bishop of Cebù in 1857.[60] Consequently, the bishop's own chapel could be a proper place for conferring Sacred Orders, even on Holy Saturday, provided it was not a general ordination that was held.

Innocent XIII, in 1723, directed a constitution to Spain. In it he treated of the restoration of ecclesiastical discipline. In one section he spoke of the relationship between ordinaries and regulars with regard to dimissorial letters, but there was mention also of the rules for the place of ordination. He repeated the general norm that, even though regulars are exempt, they are still subject to the bishop in the matter of ordination. So he restated the rule, that the ordination of regulars was to take place in the diocese in which the monastery was located. However, if for some reason the bishop did not hold general ordinations at the stated times, then the regulars were free to receive their ordination in some other diocese. The Pope also stated that he in no way abrogated any indult, if it had been granted by the Holy See after the Council of Trent, whereby a monastery had obtained the special privilege of having its members receive their Orders from any Catholic bishop.[61] This constitution was confirmed later by Pope Benedict XIII in 1724,[62] and again in 1726,[63] and also

58 S.R.C., *Mazarien.*, 18 mart. 1702 — *Decr. Auth.*, n. 2095; *supra.* p. 35.

59 S.R.C., *Bergamen.*, 24 mart. 1744 — *Decr. Auth.*, n. 2375; *supra,* p. 35.

60 S.R.C., *Nominis Jesu,* 9 maii 1857 — *Decr. Auth.*, n. 3044; *supra,* p. 35.

61 Innocentius XIII, const. *Apostolici ministerii,* 23 maii 1723, § 17 — *Magnum Bull. Rom.*, XIII, 63; *Taurinensis Bullarum Editio,* XXI, 937; *Fontes,* n. 280.

62 Const. *In supremo,* 23 sept. 1724 § 14 — *Taurinensis Bullarum Editio,* XXII, 100; *Fontes,* n. 283.

63 Const. *Pastoralis officii,* 27 mart. 1726, § 3 — *Taurinensis Bullarum Editio,* XXII, 342; *Fontes,* n. 292.

by Pope Benedict XIV in 1747.[64]

Benedict XIV also issued a letter to the suburbicarian Cardinal Bishops, and treated of the place for ordination in an incidental way. The main point he wished to establish was that these cardinals could not confer Orders in their chapels in Rome without the permission of the Vicar of Rome, which prescript is of course in accordance with the decree of the Council of Trent that had forbidden bishops to exercise pontifical functions outside their diocese without permission.[65] The Pope forbade the conferring of Major Orders in these chapels as being contrary to the Tridentine decree, but he allowed a private ordination with the proper permission. Therefore, as a general rule, the chapels of the suburbicarian cardinal bishops did not serve as proper places for the conferring of Sacred Orders[66]

There remains to be treated the question of the place for the conferring of Major Orders when the ordination was to be repeated absolutely or conditionally for some reason. Numerous decrees of the Holy Office, and some from the Sacred Congregation of Rites, indicated that such an ordination to Sacred Orders could be celebrated in any place within the diocese, inclusive of the bishop's private oratory.[67]

Finally, if a bishop was set over two dioceses which still continued distinct one from the other, then he could at his own pleasure select either of these as the place for ordination to Sacred Orders.[68]

64 Const. *Impositi Nobis,* 27 febr. 1747 — *Benedicti XIV Bullarium* (3 vols. in 4, Prati, 1845-1847), Tom. II, 164-170; *Fontes,* n. 376.

65 Sess. VI, *de ref.,* c. 5 — Schroeder, *Canons and Decrees of the Council of Trent,* pp. 50, 327; *supra,* p. 29.

66 Benedictus XIV, ep. *Ad audientiam,* 15 febr. 1753 — *Benedicti XIV Bullarium,* Tom. III, 51-56; *Fontes,* n. 424.

67 S.R.C., *Taurinen.,* 16 iun. 1837 — *Decr. Auth.,* n. 2767; *Fontes,* n. 5890; *Vivarien.,* 22 maii 1841 — *Decr. Auth.,* n. 2836; *Fontes,* n. 5913; S.C.S.Off. (Cochinchin.), 19 aug. 1851 — *Collectanea,* I, n. 1066; *ASS,* XXV (1892), 579; *Fontes,* n. 917; (Angliae), 7 sept. 1892 — *Collectanea,* II, n. 1811; *Fontes,* n. 1160; (Vic. Ap. Hong Kong), 7 maii 1902 — *Collectanea,* II, n. 2140; *Fontes,* n. 1259.

68 S.C.C., *Viterbien. et Tuscanen.,* 11 ian. 1783; *Thesaurus,* LII, 1; Gasparri, *De Sacra Ordinatione,* I, n. 101.

In summary, then, with reference to general ordinations the law concerning the place for the conferring of Major Orders designated the cathedral church. Some other church outside the episcopal city, preferably the more important one of the district, could be used for some reasonable cause. Private ordinations could be held in any place within the diocese. For religious, the place for ordination was the diocese within which their monastery was situated. The repetition of ordination to Sacred Orders, whether it was performed absolutely or conditionally, could take place anywhere within the diocese.

Section D. The Episcopacy

Article 1. The Time for the Consecration of a Bishop

The *Pontificale Romanum* indicated the rule regarding the time for the consecration of a bishop in its statement: "Statuta die consecrationis, quae debet esse Dominica, vel Natalitium Apostolorum, vel etiam festiva, si Summus Pontifex hoc specialiter indulserit... ."[69] Sunday has always, even from the earliest ages, been the acknowledged time for the consecration of a bishop.[70] The *Natalitium Apostolorum* (i.e., the day of the death of the Apostles), however, is now given official recognition as a proper time, although, on occasions, this had been previously done.[71] Lastly, the Pontifical directed that the consecration could be held on a feast day, but only if the Roman Pontiff allowed this day in a special case.

[69] Tit. *De Consecratione Electi in Episcopum;* Catalani, *Commentarium,* Tom. I, 292.

[70] *Supra,* pp. 2, 3, 6.

[71] Riganti (1661-1735) observed that bishops were consecrated in the course of time on the *Natalitia Apostolorum.* The reason for the selection of these feasts consisted in the fact that the bishops were truly the vicars and the successors of the Apostles. He noted the following examples of the occurrence of consecrations on the *Natalitia Apostolorum*: 1) Pelagius II (578-590) was consecrated on the feast of St. Andrew in 578; 2) St. Gregory VII (1073-1085) was consecrated on the feast of SS. Peter and Paul. The practice of consecrating a bishop on one of the *Natalitia Apostolorum* was incorporated in the Roman Pontifical as an approved time. — *Commentaria in Regulas, Constitutiones et Ordinationes Cancelariae Apostolicae* (2 vols., Coloniae Allobrogum, 1751), XXIV, § 1, n. 30; Gasparri, *De Sacra Ordinatione,* I, n. 84; Catalani, *Commentarium,* Tom. I, 293.

It is to be noted that under the *Natalitia Apostolorum* are not included the feasts of the Evangelists, St. Luke and St. Mark; nor is the feast of St. Barnabas included. This was definitely determined by the Sacred Congregation of Rites in a response sent to the Apostolic Delegation in Canada on April 4, 1913.[72] In the same response it was determined that the special indult, when granted by the Pope for the performing of a consecration on a festive day, included the feast days of precept, and also such feast days which, though now suppressed, were formerly of precept.[73]

Accordingly the time for the consecration of a bishop was any Sunday in the year, any *Natalitium Apostolorum,* or any feast day which had been especially approved by the Pope.

ARTICLE 2. THE PLACE FOR THE CONSECRATION OF A BISHOP

The Council of Trent enacted: "Consecratio vero, si extra curiam Romanam fiat, in ecclesia, ad quam promoti fuerint, aut in provincia, si commode fiere poterit, celebretur."[74] The same law was incorporated verbatim in the *Pontificale Romanum.*[75] Therefore the place for the consecration of a bishop was in the church to which he had been named, that is to say, the cathedral church. This was the usual procedure when the consecration was conferred outside of Rome. But the option for an alternative was given in that the consecration was allowed in any place within the province, and hence outside the diocese, especially if convenience was thus to be served. Gasparri noted that a strict compliance with the decree of the Tridentine Council was not always in evidence for sometimes a bishop-elect was consecrated even outside the province.[76]

Thus the law regarding the place for the consecration of a bishop was the following: The consecration occurring outside of Rome was to take place in the church to which the bishop had been named, or in the province of which the diocese was a part, particularly when some major convenience could thus be served.

72 S.R.C., *Delegationis Apostolicae Canadensis,* 4 apr. 1913 — *Decr. Auth.,* n. 4304; *Fontes,* n. 6391.

73 *Loc. cit.*

74 Sess. XXIII, de ref., c. 2 — Schroeder, *Canons and Decrees of the Council of Trent,* pp. 167, 439.

75 Tit. *De Consecratione Electi in Episcopum;* Catalani, *Commentarium,* Tom. I, 295.

76 *De Sacra Ordinatione,* I, n. 106.

PART II

CANONICAY COMMENTARY

CHAPTER IV

THE EPISCOPACY

SECTION A. THE TIME FOR THE CONSECRATION OF A BISHOP

Canon 1006, § 1. — Consecratio episcopalis conferri debet intra Missarum sollemnia, die dominico vel natalitio Apostolorum.

The Code of Canon Law retains and affirms the previous canon law on the time for the consecration of a bishop when it states that episcopal consecration must be conferred on a Sunday, or on a day which commemorates the death of an Apostle (*natalitio Apostolorum*).[1] This canon is, in fact, a verbatim restatement of the norms which are also found in the *Pontificale Romanum.*[2] The Pontifical, however, has an extra phrase, "vel etiam festiva, si Summus Pontifex hoc specialiter indulserit,"[3] which does not appear in the Code. This phrase will be commented on in due course.

[1] Can. 1006, § 1.

[2] "Statuta die consecrationis, quae debet esse Dominica, vel Natalitium Apostolorum ..." — Tit. *De Consecratione Electi in Episcopum;* "Dies habendae consecrationis debet esse Dominica, vel Natalitium sanctorum Apostolorum, ..." — Tit. *De Consecratione Plurium Electorum in Episcopos.* It is to be noted that the regulations of the *Pontificale Romanum* were reaffirmed by the Sacred Congregation of Rites, February 20, 1950. The occasion was the publication of the variations and additions to the rubrics dealing with ordination to the diaconate, the priesthood, and the episcopate. These additions and variations came as a result of Pope Pius XII's Apostolic Constitution, *Sacramentum Ordinis,* November 30, 1947, in which he determined precisely the matter and form for the Orders of diaconate, priesthood, and episcopate. The Congregation, when it made the changes, did not alter any of the norms on the time and place for the conferring of the sacrament, which silence amounts to a confimation of these particular regulations as they obtained in the past.

[3] *Loc. cit.*

The term, "Sunday", does not offer any difficulty. Augustine (1872-1943) made the observation that this term is to be interpreted strictly, and hence an episcopal consecration on a holy day of obligation during the week, or on a suppressed feast day, is not permitted without a special Apostolic indult.[4] Thus an episcopal consecration may be held on any Sunday in the year, even though some special feast may take precedence on that day. The pertinent point of the law is that the first day of the week is reserved for the consecration of a bishop. That the Mass assigned for a particular Sunday is impeded does not of itself make it possible to have an episcopal consecration on the weekday on which that Sunday Mass is first resumed. Only by indult could such a consecration occur.

Besides the Sundays of the year, the Code also directs that an episcopal consecration may be held on those feasts which commemorate the death of an Apostle (*natalitium Apostolorum*).[5] It is altogether fitting that these days should be so designated, as the Code itself calls the bishops the successors of the Apostles.[6] The phrase "*natalitio Apostolorum*" is of course to be understood in its liturgical and canonical sense, and not in its natural sense.[7] Thus, the *natalitum* is really the day of the death, when the person leaves the world and enters the kingdom of heaven.[8]

A list of these particular feasts of the Apostles, as compiled from the Roman Missal, here follows:

4 *A Commentary on the New Code of Canon Law* (8 vols., Vol. IV, 3. ed., St. Louis: Herder & Co., 1925), IV, 553 (hereafter cited *Commentary*).

5 Can. 1006, § 1; *Pontificale Romanum,* Tit. *De Consecratione Electi in Episcopum;* Tit. *De Consecratione Plurium Electorum in Episcopos.*

6 Can. 329, § 1. — "Episcopi sunt Apostolorum successores . . ."; Cappello, *Tractatus Canonico-Moralis de Sacramentis* (5 vols., Vol. IV, *De Ordine,* 2.ed., Torino: Marietti, 1947), IV, n. 564 (hereafter cited *De Ordine*).

7 Cappello, *loc. cit.;* Regatillo, *Ius Sacramentarium* (2.ed., Sal Terrae: Santander, 1949), n. 995.

8 Cappello, *loc. cit.;* Many, *Praelectiones de Sacra Ordinatione* (Parisiis: Letouzey et Ané, 1905), n. 94, 3° (hereafter cited *Praelectiones*).

1) St. Matthias — February 24
2) SS. Philip & James — May 1
3) SS. Peter & Paul — June 29
4) St. James — July 25
5) St. Bartholomew — August 24
6) St. Matthew — September 21
7) SS. Simon & Jude — October 28
8) St. Andrew — November 30
9) St. Thomas — December 21
10) St. John — December 27

From this list are excluded many other important feasts of the Apostles, such as: St. Peter's Chair at Rome (Jan. 18); Conversion of St. Paul (Jan. 25); St. Peter's Chair at Antioch (Feb. 22); St. John before the Latin Gate (May 6); Commemoration of St. Paul (June 30); Octave of SS. Peter and Paul (July 6); and St. Peter in Chains (Aug. 1). The reason for their exclusion is that they are not the *natalitia Apostolorum,* which phrase must be interpreted strictly.[10]

Since canon 1006, § 1, repeats the earlier law, it is to be understood according to the interpretation of approved authors who commented on the former law.[11] Many (1847-1922), one of the earlier authors, wanted to include the feast of St. Barnabas (June 11) as an approved day for episcopal consecration. He argued from a decree of the Sacred Congregation of Rites, July 30, 1901, which said that in liturgical matters the feast of St. Barnabas was to be preferred to other feasts by reason of his apostolic dignity.[12] Cap-

[9] *Missale Romanum ex Decreto Sacrosancti Concilii Tridentini restitutum, S. Pii V Pontificis Maximi iussu editum, aliorum Pontificum cura recognitum, a Pio X reformatum et Benedicti XV auctoritate vulgatum* (editio II, juxta typicam Vaticanam amplificata I, New York: Benziger Brothers Inc., 1942).

[10] Augustine, *Commentary,* IV, 533; Cappello, *De Ordine,* n. 564; Regatillo, *Ius Sacramentarium,* n. 995; Many, *Praelectiones,* n. 94, 3°.

[11] Can. 6, n. 2. — "Canones qui ius vetus ex integro referunt, ex veteris iuris auctoritate, atque ideo ex receptis apud probatos auctores interpretationibus, sunt aestimandi."

[12] S.R.C., 30 iul. 1901 — *ASS,* XXXIV (1901), 250; Many, *Praelectiones,* n. 94, 3°.

pello[13] and Regatillo,[14] who followed Cappello, agreed with Many, and included among the *natalitia Apostolorum* the feast of St. Barnabas, basing their assertion on the 1901 decree of the Sacred Congregation of Rites. The question, however, was definitely decided when, in 1913, the same Congregation answered the specific inquiry of the Apostolic Delegate of Canada, who asked whether an episcopal consecration could be held on the feast of St. Barnabas, Apostle. A negative response was given,[15] for the reason, perhaps, that St. Barnabas was not, strictly speaking, an apostle. Consequently, applying canon 6, n. 2, one must hold the same interpretation today, and therefore an episcopal consecration may not be held on the feast of St. Barnabas, without an apostolic indult.[16]

In liturgical matters the Evangelists are treated as Apostles, as can be seen from the type of Office and Mass which is used in the celebration of their feasts. Since St. John and St. Matthew are both Evangelists and Apostles, it is only concerning St. Luke and St. Mark that there arises the question whether or not their feasts

13 *De Ordine,* n. 564.

14 *Ius Sacramentarium,* n. 995.

15 S.R.C., Delegationis Apostolicae Canadensis, 4 apr. 1913: "Nonnulla autem dubia circa huius praescriptionis interpretationem nata sunt, quae pro opportuna solutione hic subiiciuntur; videlicet:

II. Utrum fieri possit in festo S. Barnabae apostoli? ...

Et Sacra eadem Congregatio, audito etiam Commissionis Liturgicae suffragio, re sedulo perpensa, ita respondendum censuit: ...

Ad II. Negative." — *Decr. Auth.,* n. 4304; *Fontes,* n. 6391; *Acta Apostolicae Sedis, Commentarium Officiale* (Romae, 1909-1929; Civitate Vaticana, 1929-), V. (1913), 186 (hereafter cited as *AAS*).

16 Abbo-Hannan, *The Sacred Canons, A Concise Presentation of the Current Disciplinary Norms of the Church* (2 vols., St. Louis: B. Herder Book Co., 1952), II, 155 (hereafter cited *The Sacred Canons*); Augustine, *Commentary,* IV, 533; Beste, *Introductio in Codicem* (3. ed., Collegeville: St. John's Abbey Press, 1946) p. 547; Bouscaren-Ellis, *Canon Law, A Text and Commentary* (Milwaukee: The Bruce Publishing Co., 1949) p. 391 (hereafter cited *Canon Law*); Coronata, *Institutiones Iuris Canonici, De Sacramentis Tractatus Canonicus* (3 vols., Torino: Marietti, 1943-1946), II, n. 235 (hereafter cited *De Sacramentis*); Vermeersch-Creusen, *Epitome Iuris Canonici* (6.ed, 3 vols., Mechlinae-Rome: H. Dessain, 1937-1946), II, n. 269.

(*natalitia*) are acceptable days for an episcopal consecration. Again the question has been settled quite adequately by the Sacred Congregation of Rites in the previously mentioned response to the Apostolic Delegate of Canada. In seeking a clarification of the Roman Pontifical's directions, he inquired whether a bishop may be consecrated on the feast of St. Mark (Apr. 25), or of St. Luke (Oct. 18). The Congregation answered in the negative.[17] In view of this verdict, the interpretation of the present canon must also exclude the feasts of St. Luke and St. Mark from serving as proper days for an episcopal consecration, for the reason that they are not Apostles.[18]

At times in the liturgical year one feast will take precedence, and cause the regular feast to be either commemorated, or transferred to another day. Should this concurrence happen on a *natalitium Apostolorum,* what is to be done concerning the consecration of a bishop? The solution seems to be based on whether the consecration is affixed to the day, or to the feast. It seems that, unlike Sunday, in this case the feast is what is really assigned as the proper day. Thus, should another feast supplant the celebration of the *natalitium Apostolorum* and the Apostle's feast is transferred to another day, then the episcopal consecration may take place on the day to which the *natalitium Apostolorum* has been transferred, and not on the original day.

As was mentioned in the beginning of this chapter, the Roman Pontifical indicates, in addition to the two regulations of the Code, a third possible time for the consecration of a bishop. The Pontifical states that the bishop-elect may receive his consecration also on a feast day, if the Holy Father allows it in a special case.[19] Actually,

17 S.R.C., *Delegationis Apostolicae Canadensis,* 4 apr. 1913: "I Quum Evangelistae in re liturgica Apostolis aequiparentur, quaeritur, utrum consecratio episcopalis possit fieri diebus natalitiis S. Lucae et S. Marci? ... Ad. I. — Negative." — *Decr. Auth.,* n. 4304;*Fontes, n.* 6391; *AAS,* V (1913), 186.

18 Abbo-Hannan, *The Sacred Canons,* II, 155; Augustine, *Commentary,* IV, 533; Beste, *Intruductio in Codicem,* p. 547; Bouscaren-Ellis, *Canon Law,* p. 391; Cappello, *De Ordine,* n. 564; Regatillo, *Ius Sacramentarium,* n. 995; Vermeersch-Creusen, *Epitome Iuris Canonici,* II, n. 269.

19 "... vel etiam festiva, si Summus Pontifex hoc specialiter indulserit ..." — Tit. *De Consecratione Electi in Episcopum;* Tit. *De Consecratione Plurium Electorum in Episcopos.*

this enactment of the Pontifical is nothing more than a concrete statement and acknowledgement of the fact that the Holy See may grant a dispensation, so that the consecration could be administered on a day other than those mentioned in the Code. Whether or not the feast day (*festiva*) referred to in the Pontifical must be of a certain rank is not stated.

Cappello points out that the Holy See will permit, by way of dispensation, a consecration on a holy day of obligation, but he does not give any further explanation.[20] The aforementioned response of the Sacred Congregation of Rites to the Apostolic Delegate of Canada affirms that a special indult of the Holy Father is needed, in order that an episcopal consecration may occur on a holy day of obligation, or also on a suppressed holy day, which occurs during the week.[21] Bouscaren-Ellis also state the necessity of an apostolic indult, in order that a holy day of obligation, actual or suppressed, may serve as a proper time for an episcopal consecration.[22]

From such statements one might be led to believe that the Holy See, in granting this special dispensation, does so only for an actual or suppressed holy day of obligation. Such, however, is not the case, as the cited authors are merely pointing out that holy days, also when suppressed, are not equal to Sundays in this regard, and so are not proper times for episcopal consecration. To say that only for these days will the Holy See grant a dispensation would be unwarrantably suggesting limits on the dispensing power of the Holy See. There is no statement to the effect that the Holy See intends to limit itself to these days alone. Consequently, the word *festiva* of the Pontifical is to be given a broad interpretation, so that practically any day may, by dispensation, become a time for the consecration of a bishop. Naturally, only the Holy See is competent to grant this type of dis-

[20] Cappello, *De Ordine,* n. 564.

[21] S.R.C., *Delegationis Apostolicae Canadensis,* 4 apr. 1913; "III. Utrum speciale indultum Summi Pontificies requiratur ad consecrationem episcopalem peragendam diebus festivis infra hebdomadam

a) qui adhuc sunt de praecepto et proinde aequiparantur Dominicis,

b) vel etiam qui olim erant de praecepto, sive in festis suppressis? ... Ad III. Affirmative ad utrumque." — *Decr. Auth.,* n. 4304; *Fontes,* n. 6391; *AAS,* V (1913), 186; *Supra,* p. 51.

[22] *Canon Law,* p. 389.

pensation, and acts through the Sacred Consistorial Congregation.[23] The Code does not state specifically that this Congregation is empowered to dispense from the observance of the proper times of episcopal consecration. Since, however, the Consistorial Congregation does the principal work in proposing nominees for the office of bishop, it may be concluded that the same Congregation also treats requests for dispensations which a bishop-elect might need for his consecration.[24]

Cappello believes that this type of dispensation is rarely given by the Holy See,[25] but Naz, on the other hand, says that it is easily granted.[26] It seems that the latter is correct when he decries the ever increasing frequency in the seeking of a dispensation from the Church's law, especially for the reason of devotion only.[27] Here, at the same time, is indicated the fact that not a very urgent cause is needed for the obtaining of a dispensation. Devotion, a personal and highly relative reason, seems a sufficient consideration,[28] and so any more grave or more pressing contingency would be ample reason for seeking a dispensation from the proper times.

For the sake of completeness, it may be stated that the Ember Saturdays are not, without a special indult, proper times for the consecration of a bishop, since they are not mentioned in this part of canon 1006, § 1.

[23] Can. 248, § 2. "Ad hanc Congregation spectat ... Episcopos, Administatores Apostolicos, Coadiutores et Auxiliares Episcoporum constituendos proponere, canonicas inquisitiones seu processus super promovendis indicere actosque diligenter expendere ..."

[24] In support of this conclusion, the writer has seen a dispensation which granted a bishop-elect the favor of receiving his consecration outside the proper time for an episcopal consecration. This dispensation came from the Sacred Consistorial Congregation.

[25] *De Ordine,* n. 564.

[26] "... un tel indult est facilement accordé ..." — *Traité de Droit Canonique* (4 vols., Vol. II *Des Sacraments,* Charles de Clercq, Paris: Letouzey et Ané, 1947), Tome II, n. 316.

[27] "... il faut cependant désapprouver la pratique de plus en plus fréquente de la solliciter pour simple motif de dévotion à l'égard d'une autre fête que celles proposées par l'Église elle-même." — *Loc. cit.*

[28] *Loc. cit.*

The last important regulation of the Code with regard to the time for episcopal consecration is that the consecration must take place during Mass (*intra Missarum sollemnia*).[29] The expression, *intra Missarum sollemnia,* does not mean that a solemn Mass is required,[30] but only that a Mass must be said. The canon has no further restrictions, so that the Mass for the consecration of a bishop may be celebrated at any time when it is lawful to say Mass. The Code permits the celebration of Mass to begin from one hour before dawn until one hour after noon.[31] Therefore, an episcopal consecration may take place at any time within these limits.

Whenever a human being acts, no matter how solemn or important the occasion, there is always the possibility that an error may occur. Hence, it is possible that the consecrating bishop and his co-consecrators might either omit some important ceremony, or even make a mistake in the essential matter and form of the consecration, which would necessitate the repetition of the consecration. In such an unfortunate event, the law provides that the ceremony may be repeated, or the omitted rite supplied, absolutely or conditionally, on any day, but, of course, during Mass.[32]

It hardly seems possible that a custom contrary to the regulations on the time for the consecration of a bishop could arise. Should, perchance, such a custom exist in any diocese, then it must be discontinued, even though it be centenary or immemorial; nor may it again be permitted to rise, as all customs contrary to this law are expressly reprobated in a later paragraph of canon 1006.[33] Of course, any custom reprobated by the Code is a corruption of the law,

29 Can. 1006, § 1.

30 Regatillo, *Ius Sacramentarium,* n. 995.

31 Can. 821, § 1. — "Missae celebrandae initium ne fiat citius quam una hora ante auroram vel serius quam una hora post meridiem."

32 Can. 1007. — "Quoties ordinatio iteranda sit vel aliquis ritus supplendus, sive absolute sive sub conditione, id fieri potest etiam extra tempora ac secreto". cf. can. 950. — "In jure verba: *ordinare, ordo, ordinatio, sacra ordinatio,* comprehendunt, praeter consecrationem episcopalem, ordines enumeratos in can. 949 et ipsam primam tonsuram, nisi aliud ex natura rei ex contextu verborum executur."

33 Can. 1006, § 5. — "Reprobatur consuetudo contra ordinationum tempora praecedentibus paragraphis praescripta..."

which the legislator not only wants corrected, but also completely rejects as a future possible custom,[34] inasmuch as he withdraws whatever consent is necessary for the emergence of any custom as having the force of law.[35]

Furthermore, the Sundays and the feasts of an apostle's death are the proper times for episcopal consecration when, by apostolic indult, an Oriental is consecrated by Latin bishops, or a Latin is consecrated by Oriental bishops.[36] In these cases the Orientals are obliged to follow the law of the Code, as they are positively included.

Finally, it is important to note that the norms for the time of episcopal consecration in no way affect the validity of the consecration. The law itself appends no invalidating clause, nor uses even an implied expression of invalidity.[37] Consequently, the non-observance of the law, even though the consecration should take place outside of Mass would not render the episcopal consecration invalid, though such a procedure would of course be gravely unlawful.

Section B. The Place for the Consecration of a Bishop

The Code does not enact any express rule with regard to the proper place wherein an episcopal consecration is to be held. At the same time, the Code does not expressly abrogate the pre-existing liturgical regulations on this matter. Hence, the pre-Code norms on

[34] Can. 5. — "Vigentes in praesens contra horum statuta canonum consuetudines sive universales sive particulares, si quidem ipsis canonibus expresse *reprobentur,* tamquam iuris correptelae corrigantur, licet sint immemorabiles, neve sinantur in posterum, reviviscere..."; can. 27, § 2. "Consuetudo quae in iure expresse reprobatur, non est rationabilis."

[35] Can. 25. — "Consuetudo in Ecclesia vim legis a consensu competentis Superioris ecclesiastici unice obtinet."

[36] Can. 1006, § 5. — "...quae servanda quoque sunt, cum Episcopus latini ritus ordinat ex apostolico indulto clericum ritus orientalis aut contra."

[37] Can. 11. — "Irritantes aut inhabilitantes eae tantum leges habendae sunt, quibus aut actum esse nullum aut inhabilem esse personam expresse vel aequivalenter statuitur."

the place for the consecration of a bishop are to be followed.[38] Therefore, it is necessary to look to the Roman Pontifical for a direction regarding the place for the consecration of a bishop. The Pontifical, which restates the law of the Council of Trent, states that the consecration, if done outside of the Roman Curia, is to be celebrated in the church to which the bishop-elect has been appointed, or in the province, if convenience can thus be served.[39] If there is more than one to be consecrated, then the Pontifical directs that the place is the church to which the one in preferred rank (*dignior*) among the bishops-elect is promoted, or in his province, if convenience can thus be served.[40] The Pontifical does not mention how the (*dignior*) is to be determined. The precriptions of can. 106, n. 3, may serve, by way of analogy, for the settling of which of two or more bishops-elect is the one in preferred rank (*dignior.*).[41]

The first choice of place, then, for the episcopal consecration is the cathedral church of the diocese to which the bishop has been appointed, unless the consecration is in Rome itself. If this rule cannot be followed for some reason, even a slight one, then the consecration may be held at any place within the province. Even this

[38] Can. 2. — "...Quare omnes liturgicae leges vim suam retinent, nisi earum aliqua in Codice expresse corrigatur."

[39] "Consecratio, si extra curiam Romanum fiat, in Ecclesia, ad quam promoti fuerint, aut in provincia, si commode fieri poterit, celebretur." — Tit. *De Consecratione Electi in Episcopum*; Conc. Trident., Sess. XXIII, *de ref.*, c. 2 — Schroeder, *Canons and Decrees of the Council of Trent,* pp. 167, 439; Noldin-Schmitt, *Summa Theologiae Moralis* (26. ed., Oeniponte, Lipsae: Sumptbus et Typis Feliciani Rauch, 1940), III, n. 476, 1.

[40] "Consecratio, si extra curiam Romanam fiat, in Ecclesia, ad quem dignior ex Electis consecrandis promotus fuerit, aut in illius provincia, si commode fieri poterit, celebretur." — Tit. *De Consecratione Plurium Electorum in Episcopos.*

[41] Can. 106, n. 3. — "Inter diversas personas ecclesiasticas quarum nulla habeat in alias auctoritatem: qui ad gradum potiorem pertinent, praecedunt eis qui sunt inferioris gradus; inter eiusdem gradus personas sed non eiusdem ordinis, qui altiorem ordinem tenet, praecedit iis qui in inferiore sunt positi; si denique ad eundem gradum pertineant eundemque ordinem habeant, praecedit qui prius est promotus ad gradum; si eodem tempore promoti sint, senior ordinatione, nisi iunior ordinatus fuerit a Romano Pontifice; et si eodem tempore ordinem receperint, senior aetate."

latter rule would not have to be followed, if it became inconvenient to do so. Hence, as the Pontifical clearly indicates, the slightest of all causes, convenience, is sufficient to have the consecration celebrated in some other place. Since only the simple direction, "if convenience can be served", is found in the Pontifical with no further restriction, the phrase is to be interpreted in such a way that what is to be considered is the convenience of the bishop-elect, or of the consecrator, or of the co-consecrators, or perhaps even the convenience that needs to be provided for those who will attend the consecration. It seems that it is left to the judgment of the bishop-elect to determine whether it is convenient to hold the consecration in the cathedral church to which he has been appointed, or in that province, or in some other place. When there is more than one to be consecrated, it seems that the judgment on the matter of convenience is left to the bishop in preferred rank (*dignior*), since the Pontifical itself gives priority of place to the church to which the *dignior* is promoted.[42] In equity, the *dignior* should consult with the other bishops-elect, and, when he makes his choice, he should take into consideration any inconvenience which the other bishops-elect might suffer. If there is a conflict and neither wishes to accede to the other, then the practical solution would lie in each one's selecting his own place for exclusively his own consecration.

All that has been said up to this point has reference to a residential bishop. What, then, is to be done in the case of an auxiliary bishop? If it is a coadjutor with the right of succession, then it seems that with regard to the place he should follow the rules already mentioned. Hence, his place of consecration, if outside of Rome, would be the cathedral of the diocese to which he is assigned as coadjutor, or within that province, if convenience can thus be served. The place, certainly, would not be his titular see. A coadjutor without the right of succession, an auxiliary, should be consecrated, not in his titualr see, but in the cathedral of the bishop to whom he has been assigned as auxiliary, or in that province, if convenience can thus be served.[43]

[42] Tit. *De Consecratione Plurium Electorum in Episcopos.*

[43] *Pontificale Romanum,* Tit. *De Consecratione Electi in Episcopum.*

Finally, it may be noted that any place which is under a general or particular local interdict is not a proper place for the holding of an episcopal consecration.[44]

[44] Can. 2270, § 1. — "Interdictum locale sive generale sive particulare ... prohibet in loco quolibet divinum officium vel sacrum ritum..."

CHAPTER V

THE MAJOR ORDERS

SECTION A. THE TIME FOR THE CONFERRING OF THE MAJOR ORDERS

ARTICLE 1. THE ORDINARY TIME FOR CONFERRING MAJOR ORDERS

Canon 1006, § 2. — Ordinationes in sacris celebrentur intra Missarum sollemnia sabbatis Quatuor Temporum, sabbato ante dominicam Passionis, et Sabbato Sancto.

The law which regulates the proper time for the conferring of the Sacred or Major Orders[1] has been consistently restated, and has remained unchanged for many centuries. The Code, therefore, merely continues the previous regulation, when it states that ordinations to Sacred Orders are to be celebrated during Mass on the four Ember Saturdays, on the Saturday before Passion Sunday, and on Holy Saturday.[2] These six days are likewise designated by the Roman Pontifical as the ordinary time for the reception of Major Orders.[3] Thus, when a bishop wants to ordain a candidate to the priesthood, or diaconate, or subdiaconate, he is obliged to select one of the six enumerated Saturdays for the ceremony, unless, as will be seen later, he has a grave reason for choosing one of the extraordinary times, or has an apostolic indult that allows him to proceed to the contrary.

The selection of one of the six proper Saturdays is left to the discretion of the bishop who is to ordain, but he must be guided by the norms of Canon Law, which demand that certain requirements be fulfilled before a candidate may be advanced to Orders, for

[1] Can. 949. — "In canonibus qui sequuntur, nomine ordinum *maiorum* vel *sacrorum* intelliguntur presbyteratus, diaconatus, subdiaconatus..."

[2] Can. 1006, § 2.

[3] "Tempora ordinationum sunt: Sabbato in omnibus Quatuor Temporibus, Sabbatum ante Dominicam de Passione, et Sabbatum Sanctum." — Tit. *De Ordinibus Conferendis.*

example: necessary age;[4] due knowledge;[5] observance of the interstices.[6]

Ordinarily, therefore, Sacred Orders are to be conferred only on the six days which have been mentioned.

Furthermore, canon 1006, § 2, directs that the Major Orders must be given during the celebration of Mass.[7] Although it would be gravely unlawful, an ordination to Sacred Orders outside of Mass would nevertheless be valid. It may be noted that it is not of the essence of the sacrament that it be given during Mass, but this rule of liturgy is of such antiquity and of customary observance that the Holy See never dispenses from it.[8] Also, it may be noted that the Mass does not need to be a Solemn Mass, for a Low Mass will suffice. Finally, the ordination ceremony may take place at any time when the law permits Mass to be said, that is, with the Mass beginning at any time from one hour before dawn until one hour after noon.[9]

Article 2. The Extraordinary Times for Conferring Majors Orders

a) — The times

Can. 1006, § 3. — Gravi tamen causa interveniente, Episcopus potest eas habere etiam quolibet die dominico aut festo de praecepto.

The Canonical legislation regarding the time for sacred ordinations received further development when the Code incorporated a new norm under canon 1006, § 3. Up to that time a dispensation, except in rare cases, was needed in order to hold an ordination to Major Orders outside the appointed times, that is, on days other than the six Saturdays mentioned above.[10] Gasparri, in commenting on

[4] Can. 975.

[5] Can. 976.

[6] Can. 978.

[7] "...intra Missarum sollemnia..."

[8] Benedictus XIV, *De Synodo Dioecesana,* Lib. VIII, cap. XI, n. 5-7; Gasparri, *De Sacra Ordinatione,* I, n. 61.

[9] Can. 821, § 1.

[10] *Supra,* pp. 60-61.

the pre-Code law listed but two occasions when a dispensation was not necessary for an ordination to Sacred Orders *extra tempora,* namely: first, if some one was elected Roman Pontiff, and he did not have these Orders; and, second, if on one of the proper Saturdays, because of the large number to be ordained or for some other urgent reason (e.g., sudden illness of the ordaining bishop), the ordination could not be completed, then on the following Sunday the rest could be ordained. He added that perhaps it could also happen, if everything was prepared for the ordination, and the bishop could not begin it for some reason, such as sickness. Since it would have entailed a grave inconvenience to defer the ordination to some other canonical time, and also for the reason that an ecclesiastical law could lose its binding force in the presence of grave inconvenience, the ordination could be held outside the stated times.[11] As is obvious, these cases were not of frequent occurrence, but still other grave reasons could be present to warrant the celebration of an ordination *extra tempora.* In such events the only solution was the bishop's seeking a dispensation from the Holy See. In order to facilitate matters the Code has now established extraordinary times for the conferring of Sacred Orders. The law now states that a bishop may hold ordinations to Major Orders on any Sunday or also on any holy day of obligation, when a grave reason is present.

Any Sunday of the year is the first of the extraordinary times for the conferring of Major Orders. This norm is clear and needs no comment. Since Sunday has been made an extraordinary time, the bishop has, under certain conditions, a larger number of days for holding ordinations to Sacred Orders.

The second of the extraordinary times is any holy day of obligation. Some discussion has taken place with regard to the interpretation of the meaning of "holy day of obligation" (*festo de praecepto*). The main question was whether the suppressed holy days were included as days for sacred ordination. The problem was treated ex-

[11] *De Sacra Ordinatione,* I n. 67; Reiffenstuel, *Jus Canonicum Universum,* Lib. I. tit. XI, n. 36; *supra,* p. 39.

pressly in *The Ecclesiastical Review,* October, 1921,[12] and in the *Perfice Munus,* April, 1926.[13] In both of these treatments the writers came to the conclusion that the suppressed holy days were included. This was also the opinion in general of the authors at that time.[14] Their main argument was drawn from two responses of the Sacred Congregation of Rites. This Congregation, in 1831, had affirmatively stated to the Bishop of Marsi that a bishop who had the faculty of conferring Sacred Orders on feast days could do so also on those feast days which had been suppressed by the Holy See.[15] Again, in 1843, there was an affirmative answer to the Bishop of Le Puy-en-Velay on two specific suppressed holy days, and at the same time the Congregation referred him to its earlier response.[16]

In opposition to this practically common opinion were Vermeersch-Creusen. They stated that, since canon 1006. § 3, did not read *"festo de praecepto etiam suppresso",* as does canon 339, § 1 (where the law treats of the obligation of applying the *Missa pro populo*), the suppressed holy days were not included. Rather, Vermeersch-Creusen interpreted the canon as including only those holy days which actually exist in the Code, even though in some particular territory by apostolic indult they are not observed.[17]

[12] Cases and Studies: "Day for Conferring Sacred Orders" — *The American Ecclesiastical Review* (Vols. I-XXXII, Philadelphia, 1889-1905; from 1905: *The Ecclesiastical Review,* Philadelphia, 1905-1943; from 1944, *The American Ecclesiastical Review,* Washington, D.C., Vol. CX, 1944-), LXV (1921), 423-425 (hereafter cited *AER* and *ER* respectively).

[13] C. Lardone, "Il tempo delle Sacre Ordinazioni" *Perfice Munus* (Torino, 1926-), I (1926), 240-241.

[14] Blat *Commentarium Textus Codicis Iuris Canonici* (6 vols., Romae: Ex Typographia Pontificia in Instituto Pii X, 1919-1927), III, Pars I, n. 388 (hereafter cited *Commentarium*) ; Genicot-Salsmans, *Theologiae Moralis Institutiones* (6. ed., 2 vols., Bruxellis, 1909), II, n. 433; Cappello, *De Ordine,* n. 564.

[15] S.R.C., *Marsorum,* 12 nov. 1831 — Decr. Auth., n. 2682; *Fontes,* n. 5858; *supra,* p. 31.

[16] S.R.C., *Anicien.,* 18 febr. 1843 — *Decr. Auth.,* n. 2852; *Fontes,* n. 5915; *supra,* p. 32.

The difference of opinion was resolved authoritatively in 1936 by the Pontifical Commission for the Authentic Interpretation of the Code. The Commission was asked whether feasts which had been suppressed by the Code for the universal Church came under expression *"festo de praecepto"* of canon 1006, § 3. The answer was in the negative.[18] Therefore, the suppressed holy days of obligation are not legitimate times for holding ordinations to Sacred Orders, even when there is present a grave reason.[19]

Since the Code Commission rendered its decision, the interpretation of *"festo de pracepto"* implies that under this phrase are included the ten holy days of obligation for the universal Church, which

[17] *Epitome Iuris Canonici,* II, n. 269, 2.

[18] Emi Patres Pontificiae Commissionis ad Codicis Canones authentice interpretandos, propositis in plenario coetu quae sequuntur dubiis, responderi mandarunt ut infra ad singula:...

II. De Tempore Ordinationis

D. An sub verbis *festo de praecepto,* de quibus in canone 1006, § 3, veniant etiam festa per Codicem in universa Ecclesia suppressa?

A. Negative.

Datum Romae, e Civitate Vaticana, die 15 mensis Maii, anno 1936. — *AAS,* XXVIII (1936), 210; J. Pauwels, "In alterum responsum De Tempore Sacrae Ordinationis", *Periodica de Re Morali, Canonica, Liturgica* (Brugis, 1927-1936; Romae, 1937—), XXV (1936), 207-208 (hereafter cited *Periodica*); Bouscaren, *The Canon Law Digest* (2 vols. and Supplement through 1948, Milwaukee, Wis.: The Bruce Publishing Co., 1934-1943-1949), II, 248 (hereafter cited *Canon Law Digest*).

[19] Crnica, *Commentarium Theoretico-Practicum Codicis Iuris Canonici* (2 vols., Šibenik: Typis Typographiae "Kačić", 1940-1941), II, Pars I, 153 (hereafter cited *Commentarium*); Vermeersch-Creusen, *Epitome Iuris Canonici,* II, n. 269,2; *Periodica,* XXV (1936), 207-208; F. Roberti, "Comment on decree of the Code Commission", *Apollinaris* (Romae, 1928—), IX (1936), IX (1936), 590-592; Cappello, *Summa Iuris Canonici* (3 vols., Vol. I and II, 4.ed., 1945; Vol. III, 2.ed., 1940, Romae: Universitas Gregoriana), II, n. 289, 2 (hereafter cited *Summa*); Regatillo, *Ius Sacramentarium,* n. 995.

are listed in canon 1247, § 1.[20] Any one of these ten holy days is an extraordinary time for conferring Major Orders, even though in some place by apostolic indult the holy day is not observed, as for example the Feast of Corpus Christi, or of SS. Peter and Paul, or of the Epiphany, or of St. Joseph in the United States.

If, however, a holy day of obligation together with its office is by special apostolic indult transferred to a Sunday, ordinations to Major Orders may be held on that Sunday, but not on the *dies a quo,* provided, of course, there is present a grave reason. [21] This interpretation is in accord with a response of the Sacred Congregation of Rites to the Administrator of the Diocese of Quebec, which response has already been mentioned in the historical treatment.[22]

It is to be noted that privileges which permit ordinations *extra tempora* were always understood in such a way that the Major Orders could be conferred only on a holy day of obligation, unless there was an explicit permission for other days.[23]

Authors benignly interpret the privileges held by some so as to include the suppressed holy days.[24] Perhaps the reason for the broader interpretation is that, since privileges which were granted before the Code, were not revoked by the Code, and still were in use up to the advent of the Code, continue in force, these privileges should be interpreted as they were rightfully interpreted at the time

20 Can. 1247, § 1. — "Dies festi sub praecepto in universa Ecclesia sunt tantum: Omnes et singuli dies dominici, festa Nativitatis, Circumcisionis, Epiphaniae, Ascensionis et sanctissimi Corporis Christi, Immaculatae Conceptionis et Assumptionis Almae Genetricis Dei Mariae, sancti Ioseph eius sponsi, Beatorum Petri et Pauli Apostolorum, Omnium denique Sanctorum."

21 Augustine, *Commentary,* IV, 534.

22 *Supra,* p. 37.

23 S.C.C., *Tirasonen.,* 11 maii 1782 — *Thesaurus,* LI, 64; Pallottini, XVI, 152, n. 16.

24 Cappello, *Summa,* II, n. 289; Coronata, *De Sacramentis,* II, n. 240; Crnica, *Commentarium,* II, Pars I, 153; Vermeersch-Creusen, *Epitome Iuris Canonici,* II, n. 269, 2.

of their grant.[25] The earlier understanding comprehended the suppressed holy days as proper times, and in virtue of canon 4 this broad view may still be followed. Naturally, privileges which allow ordinations on successive days, or on feasts of double rank, or even on ferial days, are to be understood according to the wording of the respective rescript.

b) — The condition required for the use of the extraordinary times

Since the Sundays of the year and the holy days of the universal Church are extraordinary times for ordinations to Sacred Orders, it is but natural to expect that some canonical requirement must be met before the bishop may avail himself of the grant given by the Code. There is only one such condition which is demanded by the Code, and that is the presence of a grave reason.[26] It is the bishop who is to judge whether or not the reason adduced is sufficiently grave for him to use one of the extraordinary times.[27] When the bishop makes his judgement, he should not only consider those events which affect him, but also should take into account matters and circumstances which touch the person or persons to be ordained, or even any other particular circumstance which may warrant the use of a Sunday or a holy day of obligation for sacred ordinations.[28] In arriving at his decision concerning the presence of a grave reason, the bishop needs to do no more than to make a moral estimation that such a grave cause is present; that is, his judgment is to be made in accord with ordinary prudence.[29]

Coronata states that, since the Code mentions the bishop, and not "the ordinary of the place," the faculty of using the extraordinary times does not belong to the vicar general or to the vicar capitular

[25] Can. 4. — "... itemque privilegia atque indulta quae, ab Apostolica Sede ad haec usque tempora personis sive physicis sive moralibus concessa, in usu adhuc sunt nec revocata, integra manent, nisi huius Codicis canonibus expresse revocentur."

[26] Can. 1006, § 3. "Gravi tamen causa interveniente,..."

[27] Augustine, *Commentary,* IV, 533-534; Beste, *Intruductio in Codicem,* p. 547; Bouscaren-Ellis, *Canon Law,* p. 391; Cappello, *De Ordine* n. 564, 2.

[28] Cappello, *loc. cit.; Summa,* II, n. 289,2.

[29] Cappello, *loc. cit.*

(administrator), but they should rather submit the reason to the judgment of their own bishop, or, if their proper bishop is not available for some reason, then the right belongs to the ordaining bishop.[30] When a bishop confers Major Orders in a diocese other than his own, then the judgment of the gravity of the reason to permit the use of the extraordinary times rests with the bishop of the diocese where the ordination is to take place. The reason for this is based on the fact that in conferring Major Orders a bishop must use the pontificals,[31] and to do so in another diocese required the permission of the bishop of that diocese.[32] Hence, when a bishop grants the required permission, he must at the same time take into consideration any cause demanding an extraordinary time, and render his decision on the sufficient gravity of the reason adduced. If, after the permission has been granted and the bishop of the diocese is unavailable, only then may the ordaining bishop judge whether there is present a cause sufficiently grave to invoke the use of the extraordinary times.[33]

In order that one may better understand just how grave a cause is necessary, the authors list some examples. Thus, Cappello gives as grave reasons: the departure of the bishop from the diocese for a notable time; sickness of the bishop himself, or of the candidate for Orders; or the need of priests in the diocese.[34] Another author, Crnica, enumerates the following: when Major Orders are to be conferred at the end of the scholastic year or course of theology, at which time none of the proper days occurs; or when the bishop is prevented from conferring Orders on the assigned day; or when the bishop confers Orders on Regulars who have the privilege of receiving Major Orders *extra tempora,* then others may also share in this privilege.[35] Other examples of causes as found in Coronata are: when some one is under constraint to receive the Order of priesthood with a view to furnishing his service in a benefice or ministering in a chaplaincy to which he has been appointed for life; when the dispen-

[30] *De Sacramentis,* II, n. 237.

[31] *Pontificale Romanum,* Tit. *De Ordinibus Conferendis.*

[32] Can. 1008.

[33] Coronata, *De Sacramentis,* II, n. 237.

[34] *De Ordine,* n. 564, 2; *Summa,* II, 289, 2; Bouscaren-Ellis, *Canon Law,* p. 391.

[35] *Commentarium,* II, Pars, I, 153.

sation is asked for the solace of parents who are over fifty years of age; or if it be sought by a person who is endowed with special qualities.[36]

Therefore, when these circumstances or other like reasons are present, then a bishop can safely judge that he has a grave reason, and accordingly he may proceed to confer Major Orders on a Sunday or a holy day of obligation.

Article 3. The Time for Re-Ordination

It is clear that there is a large number of candidates for the Orders of the priesthood, the diaconate and the subdiaconate. With an increase in number there is the concomitant increase in the possible danger that some order might be conferred invalidly, or that some rite might be omitted through inadvertence or carelessness. No matter what may be the source of these undesired events, many cases have in the course of time been referred to the Holy Office, or to the Sacred Congregation of Rites. As has been noted in the historical synopsis, these Congregations have always directed that the re-ordination, or the supplying of ceremonies, be undertaken at any time.[37] This same procedure is enacted into law by the Code, when it states that whenever an ordination must be repeated or some rite supplied, whether absolutely or conditionally, this ceremony can be performed outside the proper times (*extra tempora*).[38]

The expression "also outside the proper times" (*extra tempora*) is given the broadest interpretation by all the authors, so that the re-ordination or the supplying of a ceremony may take place even on liturgical feasts of the lowest rank or also on ferial days.[39] This unlimited option is altogether fitting, since any reasonable doubt in the mind of the ordaining bishop, or of the candidate, should be allayed as quickly as possible; and the best possible certainty on the validity of the ordination should exist, in order that the validity of future acts

36 *Dc Sacramentis,* II, n. 237.

37 *Supra*, pp. 36-40; cf. also Bouscaren, *Canon Law Digest,* II, 240-247.

38 Can. 1007. — "Quoties ordinatio iteranda sit vel aliquis ritus supplendus, sive absolute sive sub conditione, id fieri potest etiam extra tmepora"

39 Augustine, *Commentary,* IV, 566; *Bouscaren-Ellis,* Canon Law, p. 392; Cappello, *De Ordine,* n. 565, 4; Summa, II, n. 289,4; Coronata, *De Sacramentis,* II, n. 241; Regatillo, *Ius Sacramentarium,* n. 995.

of Orders may be assured. Thus the Code has included this special norm, whereby any re-ordination may take place as soon as possible and on any day.

When a re-ordination is held, it is permissable that on the same day, even *extra tempora,* both Major and Minor Orders together may be conferred.[40] This statement, however, does not mean that others who are to receive a major order for the first time (i.e., not by re-ordination) may be ordained together with those who are being re-ordained *extra tempora.* The authors who make this statement are speaking only of cases in which there was doubt about an ordination, and merely wanted to observe that it was possible to re-ordain at the same time many who were doubtful of their ordination.[41]

Article 4. Customs Contary to the Time for Sacred Ordination

The historical development of the law on the time for ordinations to Sacred Orders clearly shows that the legislator has always been most solicitous that the law be scrupulously observed, and not deviated from in the slightest degree without special indult. The solicitude for the observance of this particular law is again in evidence from the fact that the legislator expressly reprobates any custom which is contrary to the norms enacted for the conferring of Sacred Orders. Hence, if any contrary custom existed when the Code made its appearance, that custom may no longer be continued, even though it was a centenary or immemorial custom at that time.[42] Furthermore, the reprobated custom may never again be revived,[43] nor may any new contrary custom be introduced, for a reprobated custom is not a reasonable one, and consequently stands deprived of

40 "Insuper si ob solum dubium Ordinatio sub conditione iteretur, id a quovis Episcopo fieri potest; et tunc poterunt eodem die simul conferri Ordines tam maiores quam minores, adhibitis solis caeremoniis certo et probabiliter necessariis ad valorem." — Aertnys-Damen, *Theologia Moralis* (16.ed., 2 vol., Taurini: Marietti, 1950), II, n. 567; St. Alphonsus Liguori, *Theologia Moralis,* Lib. VI, n. 759; Coronata, *De Sacramentis,* II, n. 241.

41 *Loc. cit.*

42 Can. 5.

43 *Loc. cit.*

the consent of any ecclesiastical superior.[44] This law holds even though the custom was one observed by religious. Thus, if some religious institute had a custom contrary to the law on the proper times for the conferring of Sacred Orders, then that custom must be abandoned, or a special apostolic indult must be obtained in order that the custom may continue in effect.

It is to be noted that the reprobation of contrary customs does not affect privileges which are contrary to the Code, provided these privileges were granted by the Holy See, were still in use at the advent of the Code, and the privileges as such were not revoked either before the Code or by the Code itself.[45] However, these privileges are to be interpreted in accordance with the norms mentioned above.[46]

Article 5. The Time for Interritual Ordination

At times there arises an occasion when it becomes necessary for a cleric of the Latin rite to receive a Major Order from the bishop of an Oriental rite, or vice-versa. Whenever a case of this nature occurs, the ordaining bishop needs an apostolic indult before he may rightfully undertake the interritual ordination. The Orientals are free to hold ordinations at any time whereas the Latins are obliged to follow definite rules. Naturally, then, when by apostolic indult a Latin bishop is to ordain an oriental cleric to Major Orders, the question will be whether or not the bishop is bound to follow the law of the Code; and the same problem will face an Oriental bishop who is to ordain a Latin. The Code authoritatively settles the matter, when it indicates that the norms as set down in the Code are to be adhered to whenever there is an interritual ordination by apostolic indult.[47]

[44] Cans. 25, 27; Cappello, *De Ordine,* n. 565, 4; Augustine, *Commentary,* IV, 535.

[45] Can. 4.

[46] *Supra,* pp. 65-66.

[47] Can. 1006, § 5 — "...quae [the rules in the first four paragraphs] servanda quoque sunt, cum Episcopus latini ritus ordinat ex apostolico indulto clericum ritus orientalis aut contra."

ARTICLE 6. DISPENSATIONS FROM THE LAW REGARDING THE TIME FOR SACRED ORDINATION

Paragraphs two and three of canon 1006 give the bishop a wide choice of times for the conferring of Major Orders. Despite these broad faculties, it is possible that a bishop may desire to confer Sacred Orders on some other day outside the times approved by law; or that the bishop does not have a grave reason which would permit his using one of the extraordinary times, a Sunday or a holy day. Under such circumstances the bishop must seek a dispensation from the law before he may hold the ordination outside the proper times. Since this law is a general law of the Church, the dispensation can be granted only by the Holy See. Whenever such a dispensation is needed, it is to be sought from the Sacred Congregation of the Sacraments, as it is this Congregation which is competent in matters relating to the discipline of the sacraments.[48] In an urgent case the bishop could use canon 81, but he must invoke this canon according to the decision of the Code Commission, as given on June 26, 1947. Thus the bishop, if time permits, must first make use of the facilities of communication which the Apostolic Delegation has with the Holy See.[49] In view of the grants of canon 1006, § 3, such urgent cases will be most rare.

ARTICLE 7. INDULT GRANTED TO THE BISHOPS OF THE UNITED STATES

The Holy See has on many occasions given indults to various dioceses and institutes, and through these indults there may be sanctioned for them, *extra tempora,* the conferring of Sacred Orders. It is not the purpose here to discuss these indults in detail, as their number is large, and it would be impossible to treat all in a short space. There is, however, one important indult that calls for mention here, and that is the indult granted by the Sacred Congregation of the Sacraments to the Bishops of the United States, May 18, 1940. The Apostolic Delegate of the United States requested, in favor of the Archbishops and Bishops of the United States, the faculty to hold

48 Can. 249.

49 *AAS,* XXXIX (1947), 374; *Canon Law Digest, Supplement through* 1948, p. 15.

sacred ordinations outside the times fixed by law, namely, on feast days of double rite of the first or second class, though not of obligation, and on some Saturdays at the close of the scholastic year. To this request the Sacred Congregation replied:

> "In the audience of May 18, 1940, His Holiness Pius XII, having heard the report of the undersigned Prefect of the Sacred Congregation of the Sacraments, and in view of the representations made by the Most Excellent Apostolic Delegate of the United States, deigned to grant to the aforesaid Archbishops and Bishops the faculty asked, for three years, subject to the observance of the provisions of law, especially the Instruction of this Sacred Congregation, December 17, 1930, regarding the testing of candidates."[50]

This faculty gave to the bishops in this country ample latitude in selecting a time for the conferring of Sacred Orders. Hence, even if a particular bishop does not have a grave reason for using one of the extraordinary times of canon 1006, § 3, he may still avail himself of this faculty and use either a feast of double rite of the first or second class (which would include all the holy days, and all but two of the suppressed holy days, namely: the Feast of St. Ann on July 26, and the Feast of St. Silvester on December 31); or one of the Saturdays at the end of the scholastic year, i.e., the last Saturdays of May or the first two Saturdays of June. It is to be observed that the faculty was granted for only three years, and consequently calls for a periodical renewal.

The latest renewal of this faculty came in the year 1952. The letter of the Apostolic Delegate by which this faculty was communicated to the bishops reads as follows:

> No. 249/40
>
> March 17, 1952.
>
> Your Excellency:
>
> In virtue of the special faculties granted by His Holiness, Pope Pius the Twelfth, the Sacred Congregation for the Discipline of the Sacraments has renewed *ad aliud*

[50] *Canon Law Digest,* II, 249.

triennium the faculty "qua sacrae Ordinationes haberi possint etiam extra tempora a iure statuta, scilicet diebus festis ritus duplicis primae vel secundae classis, quamvis non de praecepto, necnon ultimis sabbatis Maii et duobus primis sabbatis Junii, exeunte anno scholari . . . servatis de iure servandis, praesertim Instructione S. Congregationis de Sacramentis diei 27 Decembris 1930 de scrutinio."

This grant will be in force until February 20, 1955, in favor of all local Ordinaries of the United States.

In addition I am pleased to notify Your Excellency that the Holy See has also given the Most Reverend Bishops the faculty to confer Sacred Orders on each of the Saturdays of May and June for this year, and the Ordinaries who take advantage of it are asked to report the fact to the Apostolic Delegate.

With cordial regards and best wishes, I am

Sincerely yours in Christ,

✠A. G. Cicognani

Archbishop of Laodicea

Apostolic Delegate

51

The faculty as granted for 1952 was extended to include all the Saturdays of May and June. Any bishop who used this grant had to make a report to the Apostolic Delegate. For the remaining time during which the faculty will be in force, until February 20, 1955, a bishop may avail himself of the opportunity to confer Major Orders on the last Saturdays of May, possible the last two, and the first two Saturdays of June.

It is obvious, therefore, that the bishops of the United States have at their disposal a large number of days, which may be legitimately used to confer Sacred Orders. A bishop who would go beyond the law and the indult without a dispensation would indeed ordain validly, but would be acting illicitly.

51. *The Jurist* (Washington, D.C., 1941—), XIII (1952), 247.

Section B. The Place for the Conferring of the Major Orders

Article 1. The Proper Territory

Canon 1008. — Episcopus extra proprium territorium, sine Ordinarii loci licentia, nequit ordines conferre, in quorum collatione pontificalia exercentur, salvo praescripto can. 239, § 1, n. 15.

The problem of determining which is the proper place for the conferring of Sacred Orders, involves the consideration of two facts: first, the proper territory: and second, the place within the proper territory. The latter will be discussed in a following article.[52] It is the former, the proper territory, which is under consideration at this moment.

The Code does not deviate from the previous legislation, but clearly states that a bishop cannot ordain outside his own territory whenever he must use the pontificals, unless he has received the permission of the local ordinary in whose territory the ordination is to be held. This restriction holds even if the one to be ordained is a subject of the ordaining bishop. The Roman Pontifical points out that a bishop may confer the minor orders outside of Mass, when he is vested with a stole over his rochet, or surplice (if he is a Regular),[53] and simple mitre.[54] In other words, he confers the Minor Orders in this case without the "pontificals," which in law includes both the crozier and the mitre.[55] Only tonsure and the Minor Orders may be given outside of Mass, for the Major Orders must

[52] *Infra*, p. 76.

[53] Regular bishops now follow the same norm as that for other bishops, that is, Regulars use the rochet. The change in the rubric of the Pontifical was made by Benedict XV in 1930. — *AAS*, XII (1920), 149.

[54] "Quando autem Pontifex extra Missarum solemnia est promoturus aliquos ad primam Tonsuram, vel ad quatuor minores Ordines, sufficit quod habeat stolam super rochettum, vel supra superpelliceum (si sit Regularis) et mitram simplicem." — Tit. *De Ordinibus Conferendis*.

[55] Can. 337, § 2. "Exercere pontificalia in iure est sacras functiones peragere quae ex legibus liturgicis requirunt insignia pontrificalia, idest baculum et mitram." Beste, *Introductio in Codicem*, p. 541; Augustine, *Commentary*, IV, 544.

be given during Mass.[56] But when the bishop ordains at Mass he must use the pontificals, the crozier and the mitre.[57] Therefore, whenever the bishop confers Sacred Orders he is using the pontificals, and so is restricted to his own territory, unless he obtains permission to ordain in another diocese. Thus, the proper place for the conferring of Major Orders is, first of all, the territory of the ordaining bishop.

The one who gives the permission for an outside bishop to confer Sacred Orders is the local ordinary within whose territory the ordination is to be held. Thus, all those who fall under the term "local ordinary" may grant this permission, and not merely the residential bishop.[58] The vicar general, however, must not use his power contrary to the mind and will of his bishop.[59]

There is one exception to this general law, and that has to do with the privileges of cardinals. Among the many privileges listed in canon 239, § 1, is one which permits a cardinal to perform pontifical functions with the throne and canopy in all churches outside of Rome, though he will of course notify the local ordinary if he wishes to celebrate in the cathedral church.[60] Hence a cardinal could ordain a person to Sacred Orders outside his own territory, provided the other requirements of the law have been fulfilled; and he does not need the permission of the local ordinary. At most, the cardinal, when he desires to use the cathedral church, need only notify the bishop, regardless of whether or not the bishop is in favor of the ordination.[61]

Augustine observed that the suburbicarian cardinal bishops are not allowed to confer Orders in their private chapels in Rome with-

56 Can. 1006, § 2. *supra*, pp. 60-61.

57 *Pontificale Romanum*, Tit. *De Ordinibus Conferendis.*

58 Can. 198.

59 Can. 369, § 2. "Caveat ne suis potestatibus utatur contra mentem et voluntatem sui Episcopi . . ."

60 Can. 239, § 1, 15°. "Pontificalia cum throno et baldachino peragendi in omnibus ecclesiis extra Urbem, Ordinario praemonito, si ecclesia sit cathedralis."

61 Augustine, *Commentary*, IV, 544-545; Blat, *Commentarium*, III, Pars I, n. 390; Regatillo, *Ius Sacramentarium*, n. 997.

out the permission of the Cardinal Vicar.[62] This direction is found in a constitution of Benedict XIV, which has been mentioned previously.[63]

Article 2. The Place Within the Proper Territory

a) — The place for general ordinations

> Can. 1009. — § 1. Ordinationes generales in cathedrali ecclesia, vocatis praesentibusque ecclesiae canonicis, publice celebrentur; si autem in alio dioecesis loco, praesente clero loci, dignior, quantum fieri poterit, ecclesia adeatur.

The law of the Church has been most constant in regard to the place where ordinations to Sacred Orders are to be held. The law, as found in the Code, is a repetition of the decree of the Council of Trent on the same subject,[64] and of the direction set forth in the Roman Pontifical.[65] There is, however, a slight difference in the wordings. Whereas the Code has *"ordinationes generales"*, the Council of Trent and the Pontifical have *"Ordinationes sacrorum Ordinum, statutis a iure temporibus."*[66] This slight difference in wording is of importance only in helping to know what is meant by "general ordinations."

Some authors, as Cappello[67] and Regatillo, [68] understand this expression to mean an ordination ceremony in which there are many to be ordained, and all, or almost all, the orders are to be conferred.[69] Most authors, however, understand "general ordinations" to mean those that are held on the six Saturdays specified in canon 1006, § 2,

62 *Op. cit.,* IV, 545.

63 *Supra,* p. 45.

64 Sess. XXIII, *de ref.,* c. 8 — Schroeder, *Canons and Decrees of the Council of Trent,* pp. 50, 327; *supra,* p. 41.

65 Tit. *De Ordinibus Conferendis.*

66 *Loc. cit.*

67 *De Ordine,* n. 568,2; *Summa,* II, n. 290,2.

68 *Ius Sacramentarium,* n. 997, b.

69 "Dicuntur *generales ordinationes,* in quibus complures sunt ordinandi et omnes aut fere omnes conferuntur ordines." — *Loc. cit.*

at which all candidates desiring to be ordained may be present.[70]

Augustine made some further observations on thie definition. He believed that, since canon 1006, § 3, permits for a grave reason ordinations to Sacred Orders on a Sunday or a holy day of obligation, these days seem also to be included in the notion of "general ordinations". Accordingly he stated that a general ordination is one that should be held on the six Saturdays, but may be transferred to another day for a grave reason. He wrote: "But canon 1006, § 3, does not exclude the time-honored practice and view of the school that general ordinations are really only those held on the six Saturdays, because said canon only says, ordinations for higher orders may be held on a Sunday or holy day of obligation. Therefore, the bishop, ... would have to state clearly that an ordination to be held on any other day than one of the six Saturdays is a general ordination."[71] Vermeersch-Creusen concur in this interpretation.[72] Coronata inclines to the same view, but with some limitation. He considers an ordination held at the extraordinary times indicated in canon 1006, § 3, to be a general ordination only when no order is omitted and no candidate for orders is excluded.[73] This opinion, or definition, seems to be the preferred one, but the bishop should make it clear that an ordination held on a Sunday or a holy day of obligation for a grave reason is a general ordination.

Canon 1009, § 1, rules that the general ordinations are to be celebrated in the cathedral church. Thus the cathedral church is designated as the proper place within the diocese for sared ordinations. If there is no cathedral church, then the pro-cathedral is the

70 Abbo- Hannan, *The Sacred Canons,* II, 158; Augustine, *Commentary,* IV, 546; Beste, *Introduction in Codicem,* p. 547; Blat, *Commentarium,* III, Pars I, n. 391; Bouscaren-Ellis, *Canon Law,* p. 392; Coronata, *De Sacramentis,* II, n. 243; Crnica, *Commentarium,* II, Pars I, 154; Vermeersch-Creusen, *Epitome Iuris Canonici,* II, n. 270, 2; Woywod-Smith, *A Practical Commentary on the Code of Canon Law* (revised and enlarged edition, 2 vols., New York: Joseph F. Wagner, Inc., 1948), I, n. 972 (hereafter cited *A Practical Commentary*)

71 *Loc. cit.*

72 *Loc. cit.*

73 "... dummodo nullus ordo excipiatur et nullus ordinandus excludatur." — *De Sacramentis,* II, n. 243.

proper place. Also equivalent to the cathedral church is the abbatial or prelatial church of an abbot or a prelate *nullius*.[74] If a bishop is the ordinary of two dioceses, then it is left to his free choice whether the general ordinations are to be celebrated in the one or the other diocese. It is fitting, says Coronata, that the general ordinations should not always be celebrated in the same cathedral church.[75] Furthermore, it may be pointed out that it is the main altar where the general ordinations should be held, unless a reasonable cause demands otherwise.[76]

The second half of paragraph one of canon 1009 indicates that it is possible for a bishop to hold a general ordination in some other place in the diocese, but, whenever he does so, he should, in so far as it is possible, select the more important (*dignior*) church of that section of the diocese. Just how the more important church is to be determined is not stated in the canon, nor is it mentioned in the sources or the authors. Perhaps a church can be judged to be the more important one for any of the following reasons: that it is the oldest one in a particular district; or that it is the mother church of the others around it; or that it serves the greater part of the people; or that it is the largest church in the area, and so is better suited to accommodate the crowd which is usually present at an ordination ceremony; or that it outranks the other churches for any other similar reason. The bishop, however, is obliged to chose the more important church as long as that proves possible; and so any reasonable cause is sufficient for him to overlook the more important church and select another.

Since the canon allows the bishop to have general ordinations in other parts of the diocese and in a church other than the cathedral church, it may be asked what kind of reason he must have in order to hold a general ordination in some other section of the diocese, and in some other church. Paragraph one of canon 1009 is silent on the matter. The interpretation of the law of the Council of Trent, which is retained in this canon, is that the bishop needed only a

[74] Blat, *Commentarium,* III, Pars I, n. 391; cf. also can. 215, § 2.

[75] *De Sacramentis,* II, n. 243.

[76] Coronata, *loc cit.*

reasonable cause in order to select another church, or another locale.[77] The same interpretation may still be applied, so that any reasonable cause will suffice for a bishop to select some other church for a general ordination.[78] Thus, Cappello teaches that *"celebrentur"* is to be understood broadly, so that it does not imply a strict obligation, but only that it is more appropriate that the general ordination be held in the cathedral church.[79]

The importance of framing an acceptable definition of the phrase "general ordination" and of knowing what it means lies in the fact that the canons of the cathedral church must be called to attend at a general ordination and in turn must put in their presence.[80] In fact, the bishop may even threaten punishment, if the canons should refuse to attend.[81] The presence of the cathedral chapter can also be urged for a particular ordination to Sacred Orders which the bishop may hold in the cathedral church, for canon 412, § 1, demands that the canons of the cathedral church be present at all pontifical functions.[82]

In places where a cathedral chapter has not been established, as in the United States, the question may arise whether the diocesan

77 St. Alphonsus, *Theologia Moralis,* Lib. VI, 798; *supra,* p. 43.

78 Coronata, *De Sacramentis,* II, n. 243; can. 6, n. 2.

79 *De Ordine,* n. 568, 2; *Summa,* II, n. 290, 2; Regatillo, *Ius Sacramentarium,* n. 997.

80 Can. 1009, § 1; can. 412, § 1. "Canonici sive ecclesiae cathedralis sive collegialis Episcopo sollemniter Missam celebranti aut alia pontificalia exercenti, etiam in aliis ecclesiis civitatis aut suburbii, ab eodem invitati, assistere et inservire debent,..."

In explaining the scope of can. 412, the Sacred Congregation of the Council quoted can. 337, § 2, and gave an explanation of this latter canon. Under the term *"exercere pontificalia"* is the conferring of orders. Cf. S.C.C., *Resolutio, Monopolitana,* 9 febr. 1924 — *AAS,* XVII (1925), 245; *Canon Law Digest,* I, 200, 229-230.

81 Augustine, *Commentary,* IV, 547.

82 Cans. 412, § 1; 337, § 2.

83 Can. 427. — "Coetus consultorum dioecesanorum vices Capituli cathedralis, qua Episcopi senatus, supplet; quare quae canones ad gubernationem dioecesis, sive sede plena sive ea impedita aut vacante, Capitulo cathedrali tribuunt, ea de coetu quoque consultorum dioecesanorum intelligenda sunt."

consultors must be called and whether they are obliged to attend the ordination. The consultors do not have this duty, for the diocesan consultors take the place of the cathedral chapter only for the government of the diocese, and not for liturgical functions.[83]

If, however, a general ordination is celebrated in some other section of the diocese, the canons of the cathedral chapter cannot be compelled to attend; but, if the general ordination is held in some other church of the see city or its suburbs, then the canons must be present, if the bishop invited them, not, however, all of them.[84]

The clergy of the specially chosen church are not under the obligation of compulsory presence, as this obligation cannot be derived from the expression "the local clergy being present" (*praesente clero loci*).[85] Even though there is no strict obligation for the clergy to attend, nevertheless the local clergy should be present, in order that as much honor as possible may be shown to the sacrament of Holy Orders in accord with the desire of Church.[86] But, if the church which has been specifically designated has its own collegiate chapter, then the canons must be present at the ordination to Major Orders, whether it be a general or a particular ordination. They must also be present if the ordination is held in some other church of the city or its suburbs, where the collegiate chapter exists, not, however, all of them.[87]

Finally, the canon directs that general ordinations are to be celebrated publicly, that is, before the faithful. This does not mean that any special effort must be made to assure their presence, but that the faithful are not to be prohibited from attending, and that rather they should be encouraged to come to the general ordination. The

84 S.C.C., *Resolutio, Monopolitana,* 9 febr. 1924: 2. b) "If the functions are in other churches, but within the city or its suburbs, the canons are bound to assist him at his request—not however all of them, but only such a number that there will still be enough canons remaining for service in the cathedral or collegiate church itself." — *AAS,* XVII (1925), 245; *Canon Law Digest,* I, 230.

85 Can. 1009, § 1; also Augustine, *Commentary,* IV, 547.

86 Blat, *Commentarium,* III, Pars I, n. 391; Woywod-Smith, *A Practical Commentary,* I, n. 972.

87 Can. 412, § 1; S.C.C., *Resolutio, Monopolitana,* 9 feb. 1924 — *AAS,* XVII (1925), 245; *Canon Law Digest,* I, 230.

underlying reason is that the Church wants to foster among the faithful a greater respect for the priesthood (and the other Major Orders). Then, too, such has been the ancient practice of the Church, which is still in evidence in the sacred liturgy, when the people are asked to give their testimony or approval of the one to be promoted to Sacred Orders.[88]

From what has been said, the conclusion is that the proper place within the diocese for conferring Sacred Orders is the cathedral church, when there is a general ordination, that is, one held at times mentioned in can. 1006, § 2; or even some other church, the more important one of the chosen locality (to the extent this proves feasible), when there is a reasonable cause which permits the holding of a general ordination outside the cathedral church.

b) — The place for particular ordinations

> Canon 1009, § 2. — Non prohibetur autem Episcopus, iusta suadente causa, ordinationes particulares habere in aliis etiam ecclesiis itemque in oratorio domus episcopalis aut Seminarii aut religiosae domus.

Particular ordinations are those held on any day other than the six Saturdays listed in canon 1006, § 2.[89] This definition is derived from the discussion on the meaning of "general ordination," which

[88] Blat, *loc. cit.; Pontificale Romanum,* Tit. *De Ordinatione Presbyteri.* In the beginning of the ceremony the bishop addresses an admonition to the clergy and the people, which concludes: "Si quis igitur habet aliquid contra illum, pro Deo, et propter Deum, cum fiducia exeat, et dicat; verum tamen memor sit conditionis suae." A similar admonition is found in the ceremony for the diaconate, Tit. *De Ordinatione Diaconi.*

[89] Abbo-Hannan, *The Sacred Canons,* II, 158; Augustine, *Commentary,* IV, 546; Beste, *Introductio in Codicem,* p. 547; Blat, *Commentarium,* III, Pars I, n. 391; Bouscaren-Ellis, *Canon Law,* p. 392; Coronata, *De Sacramentis,* II, n. 244; Crnica, *Commentarium,* II, Pars I, 154; Vermeersch-Creusen, *Epitome Iuris Canonici,* II, n. 270, 2; Woywod-Smith, *A Practical Commentary,* I, n. 972.

appears in section a) of this article.[90] Thus, an ordination to any of the Sacred Orders in one of the extraordinary times, or on a day permitted by privilege or indult, is a particular ordination, unless, as was seen above, the ordination when held on a Sunday or on a holy day of obligation, and for a grave reason, extends to all Orders, so that no candidate is excluded, and the bishop has declared this ordination to be a general one.

Ordinarily, even for a particular ordination, the proper place within the diocese for conferring Sacred Orders is the cathedral church, or the more important church of some district, according to canon 1009, § 1. This canon, in paragraph two, allows a bishop (not however the vicar general or the vicar capitular [administrator]) and also an abbot or a prelate *nullius*[91] to hold particular ordinations in other churches of the diocese, abbacy, or prelacy, such as the oratory of the episcopal residence, the oratory of the seminary, or the oratory of a religious house, when he has a just cause for so acting.

Particular ordinations may be celebrated in other churches within the diocese, that is, in churches other than either the cathedral church, or also the more important church of a district. In other words, a particular ordination may take place in any church within the diocese. "Church", in this rule, must be understood in its canonical sense, that is, as a sacred structure devoted to divine worship for the principal purpose of being used by all the faithful for public divine worship.[92] Thus, any public oratory, semi-public oratory, or private oratory, is not a proper place for a particular ordination to Sacred Orders, unless the oratory is that of the bishop's residence, of the seminary, or of a religious house.[93]

The oratory of the bishop's residence is the chapel which the law permits a bishop to erect in his house.[94] Equivalent to the oratory of the bishop's residence is that of an abbot or a prelate *nullius*.[95] It

90 *Supra*, pp. 76-77.

91 Can. 215, § 2.

92 Can. 1161. — "Ecclesiae nomine intelligitur sedes sacra divino cultui dedicata eum potissimum in finem ut omnibus Christifidelibus usui sit ad divinum cultum publice exercendum."

93 Blat, *Commentarium*, III, Pars I, n. 391.

94 Can. 1189.

95 Blat, *loc. cit.*

is to be noted that the bishop's house (*domus episcopalis*) is the one in which the bishop habitually dwells, but the term is not to be interpreted rigidly, as custom permits the bishop to make use of a summer residence.[96] Thus, even the latter could be a proper place for a particular ordination to Sacred Orders.

The oratory of the seminary may be understood to include not only the oratory of the major seminary, but even the one in the minor seminary. The term in the canon is general, and so may be taken in its broadest sense.[97]

The religious house (*religiosae domus*) of this canon is the house of any institute, according to canon 488, n. 5.[98] Hence, as a proper place for a particular ordination to Sacred Orders may be the oratory of any religious house, whether it be the religious house of men or of women religious. Although the societies of the common life[99] are not religious institutes in a full and technical sense, nevertheless, their houses may also be included under the phrase *"religiosae domus."* Hence, the oratory in a house of some society of the common life may be a proper place for a particular ordination to Sacred Orders.

Before a bishop may designate one of these places for a particular ordination, he must have a just cause. It is not necessary that this just reason be a grave one, as even a light reason will suffice, and such a reason in practice is hardly ever lacking,[100] and so any good reason suffices for a bishop who for a particular ordination wishes to utilize any of the places mentioned in paragraph two of canon 1009.[101] Such a just cause, for example, could be sickness of the ordaining bishop or of the one to be ordained; greater conven-

96 Augustine, *Commentary,* IV, 547; Barbosa, *De Officio et Potestate Episcopi,* Pars II, Alleg. 11, n. 24.

97 Augustine, *loc. cit.*

98 Can. 488, 5°. *"Domus religiosae,* domus alicuius religionis in genere;"

99 Can. 673, § 1. "Societas sive virorum sive mulierum, in qua sodales vivendi rationem religiosorum imitantur in communi degentes sub regimine Superiorum secundum probatas constitutiones, sed tribus consuetis votis publicis non obstringuntur, non est proprie religio, nec eius sodales nomine religiosorum proprie designantur."

100 Cappello, *De Ordine,* n. 568, 3.

101 Bouscaren-Ellis, *Canon Law,* p. 393.

ience; or even for the sake of devotion.[102] Finally, it is the ordaining bishop who is to judge whether or not the reason alleged is a just one.[103]

It may also be noted that any place which is under a general or a particular local interdict is not a proper place for conferring Major Orders.[104] Some authors hold that in some extraordinary case, if sacred ministers would otherwise be lacking, and the recipients could not be sent for ordination to some other place, it might be permissible to confer sacred orders at the exceptional times mentioned in canon 2270, § 2: namely, on the feasts of Christmas, Easter, Pentecost, Corpus Christi, and the Assumption of the Blessed Virgin Mary.[105] However, it seems that in view of the express prohibition of canon 2270, § 2 the opinion of these authors lacks probability, and so this opinion is not to be folloyed.

Article 3. The Proper Place for Conferring Sacred Orders on Religious

Religious are, of course, obliged to follow the preceding norms on the place for sacred ordination, but in connection with this matter a further question arises: In which diocese are they to be ordained? Exclusive of any contrary privilege or indult which a particular religious institute may possess, the general rule is that a religious is to be ordained in that diocese in which is located the religious house to which the candidate for orders belongs. This rule is drawn from the canon which determines the bishop to whom a religious superior is to send dimissorial letters.[106] Since a religious superior usually is

[102] Crnica, *Commentarium,* II, Pars I, 154.

[103] *Loc cit.*

[104] Can. 2270, § 1. — "Interdictum locale sive generale sive particulare ... prohibet in loco quodlibet divinum officium vel sacrum ritum..."

[105] Can. 2270, § 2. "In die Nativitatis Domini, Paschatis, Pentecostes, sanctissimi Corporis Christi et Beatae Mariae Virginis in caelum assumptae interdictum locale suspenditur, et prohibetur tantum collatio ordinum et sollemnis nuptiarum benedictio."; Coronata, *Institutiones Iuris Canonici* (5 vols., Vols. I, II, 2.ed., 1939; Vol. III, 2.ed., 1941; Vol. IV, 2.ed., 1945; Vol. V, 2.ed., 1947, Taurini, Romae: Marietti), IV, n. 1789.

[106] Can. 965. — "Episcopus ad quem Superior religiosus litteras dimissorias mittere debet, est Episcopus dioecesis, in qua sita est domus religiosa, ad cuius familiam pertinet ordinandus."

not a bishop, and so does not have the power to confer Sacred Orders, he must sent his subjects to a bishop who will confer these Major Orders. When the religious superior sends his candidates for Orders to a bishop, he must also send the necessary dimissorial letters. Canon 965 determines which bishop is to receive these letters, and consequently this same canon also determines the diocese in which religious are to receive Sacred Orders, namely, the diocese wherein the religious house is situated.

It is only in the special cases mentioned in canon 966, § 1, that a religious may be ordained to Sacred Orders in a diocese other than the one where his religious house is located. Hence, if the diocesan bishop of the place where the house is situated gives his permission to the religious superior to direct the dimissorial letter to the bishop of some other diocese; if the diocesan bishop is of a different rite; if he be absent, or if he will not hold ordinations at the next proper time according to canon 1006, § 2; or when the diocese is vacant and the administrator is not a bishop, then a religious may be sent to some other diocese and there receive Sacred Orders.[107]

In these cases the bishop who will ordain must receive authentic notification from the curia of the diocesan bishop, who would ordinarily be the proper bishop, that such a reason really exists.[108] Of course, religious superiors are warned not to use fraudulent means to deprive the diocesan bishop of his right of ordaining, either by sending their subjects who are candidates for Orders to another religious house outside the diocese, or by intentionally postponing the issuance of dimissorial letters to a time when the bishop will either be absent or not have arranged a time for the conferring of orders.[109] Superiors

107 Can. 966. — § 1. "Tunc tantum Superior religiosus ad alium Episcopum litteras dimissorias mittere potest, cum Episcopus dioecesanus licentiam dederit, aut sit diversi ritus, aut sit absens, aut non sit ordinationem habiturus proximo legitimo tempore ad normam can. 1006, § 2, vel denique cum dioecesis vacet nec eam regat qui charactere episcopali polleat."

108 Can. 966. — § 2. "Necesse est ut singulis in casibus id Episcopo ordinaturo constet ex authentico Curiae episcopalis testimonio."

109 Can. 967. — "Caveant Superiores religiosi ne in fraudem Episcopi dioecesani subditum ordinandum ad aliam religiosam domum mittant aut concessionem litterarum dimissoriarum de industria in id tempus differant, quo Episcopus vel abfuturus, vel nullas habiturus sit ordinationes."

who presume to violate these prescriptions of the Code incur *ipso facto* a suspension from the celebration of Mass for a month.[110]

From the regulations of these canons, the conclusion is that, besides the other prescribed requisites on the part of the candidate, as a general rule the proper diocese where a religious is to receive Sacred Orders is the diocese in which is situated the religious house to which the candidate belongs.

110 Can. 2410. — "Superiores religiosi qui, contra praescriptum can. 965-967, subditos suos ad Episcopum alienum ordinandos remittere praesumpserint, ipso facto suspensi sunt per mensem a Missae celebratione."

CHAPTER VI

THE MINOR ORDERS

SECTION A. THE TIME FOR THE CONFERRING OF THE MINOR ORDERS

ARTICLE 1. THE PROPER DAYS FOR CONFERRING MINOR ORDERS

> Canon 1006, § 4. — "...ordines minores singulis diebus dominicis et festis duplicibus, mane tamen conferri possunt."

Although the Code retains the major part of the earlier law regarding the time for conferring Minor Orders, it does make one important change. The present law grants that minor orders may be given on Sundays and feasts of double rite, but only in the morning.[1] The Roman Pontifical contains the same regulation, except for an extra phrase, which phrase will be indicated in due course.[2]

The law has three separate norms, the first of which is that Sunday is a proper time for the conferring of Minor Orders. This enactment is sufficiently clear and raises no difficulty. Hence, a bishop may make use of any Sunday within the year to confer Minor Orders. If, however, the Sunday Mass and Office are impeded, and then resumed on a weekday, that weekday does not become a proper time for an ordination to Minor Orders.

The second statement of the law is that the Minor Orders may be conferred on feast days of double rite. It is here that the Code introduces a change, as can be seen from a comparison with the Roman Pontifical. The Pontifical states that the Minor Orders may be conferred on Sundays and on feast days of double rite which are of precept (*"festis diebus duplicibus ex praecepto"*).[3] According to

[1] Can. 1006, § 4.
[2] Tit. *De Ordinibus Conferendis; De minoribus Ordinibus.*
[3] Tit. *De Ordinibus Conferendis.*

the interpretation of the pre-Code law, the days which were mentioned in the Pontifical included both the existing and the suppressed holy days of obligation, but these holy days only.[4] Today the common interpretation of the phrase in the canon, "feasts of double rite" (*festis duplicibus*), is that they are feasts which are marked in the calendar as being of double rite, either major or minor. Only feasts which are semi-doubles or simples, and also the ferial days, are excluded from being proper days for the conferring of Minor Orders.[5] The primary reason for this interpretation is drawn from the text of the canon, which expressly and patently distinguishes "feasts of double rite" in paragraph four from "feasts of precept" in paragraph three.[6] There seems to be no other reason for using a different terminology, except that the legislator wants the term "feasts of double rite" to be understood in the general sense as indicated.[7] Therefore, any day which is of double rite is a proper time for the conferring of Minor Orders.

Since the Ember Saturdays, the Saturday before Passion Sunday, and Holy Saturday are the times usually associated with ordinations, naturally the question arises whether or not Minor Orders may be conferred on these days, even though they are not of double rite. Regatillo[8] and Romani[9] state that Minor Orders may be conferred on these days, but they give no explanation. Vermeersch-Creusen in their *Epitome Iuris Canonici*,[10] and Vermeersch again in the *Periodica*[11] concur in the interpretation which would permit ordinations

[4] *Supra*, p. 31.

[5] Abbo-Hannan, *The Sacred Canons*, II, 156; Augustine, *Commentary*, IV, 535; Bouscaren-Ellis, *Canon Law*, p. 392; Cappello, *De Ordine*, n. 565,3; *Summa*, II, 289,3; Coronata, *De Sacramentis*, II, n. 238,b; Regatillo,*Ius Sacramentarium*, n. 995; Romani, *Institutiones Juris Canonici* (2 vols. in 3, Romae: Editrice "Iustitia", 1941-1945), II, Pars I, n. 588; Vermeersch-Creusen, *Epitome Iuris Canonici*, II, n. 269,3; Woywod-Smith, *A practical Commentary*, I, n. 969.

[6] Can. 1006, § § 3, 4; Cappello, *loc. cit.*

[7] Augustine, *loc. cit.*

[8] *Ius Sacramentarium*, n. 995.

[9] *Institutiones Juris Canonici*, II, Pars I, n. 588.

[10] II, n. 269,3.

[11] "De Diebus quibus ordines minores conferre possunt," *Periodica*, XXII (1933), 136*-137*.

to Minor Orders on the six mentioned Saturdays. They base their assertion on the norms set down in the Roman Pontifical, namely: "On the Ember Saturdays, when general ordinations are held, Tonsure must be given after the *Kyrie, eleison.* Then, after the first lesson has been read, the Porters are ordained; after the second lesson, the Readers; after the third, the Exorcists; after the fourth, the Acolytes."[12] "If the ordinations are held on the Saturday before Passion Sunday, since only one lesson is read, Tonsure must be given immediately after the *Introit;* all the Minor Orders after the *Kyrie, eleison.*"[13] But if ordinations are held on Holy Saturday, . . . the Bishop says the Prayers at the Foot of the altar, and having said the *Kyrie, eleison,* for the Mass, he ordains to first Tonsure. Then he says, *"Gloria in excelsis Deo,"* and when this is finished, he ordains to the four Minor Orders."[14] From these quotations it is clear that the Pontifical envisions the conferring of Minor Orders on the six Saturdays of canon 1006, § 2, when general ordinations are held, and accordingly makes provision for their conferral.

In the *Canon Law Digest* there is found a private reply which touches on the particular point under consideration. Although the precise question is not known, the following reply, on January 20, 1941, was given by the Sacred Congregation of the Sacraments to a bishop of some country other than the United States:

> "Reply. Canon 1006, § 4, does not contain the word *tantum;* moreover, it states: *first tonsure and minor orders may be conferred,* not *must* be. Consequently, whenever

12 "In Sabbatis Quatuor Temporum, in quibus fiunt ordinationes generales, Tonsurae fieri debent post *Kyrie, eleison.* Deinde, dicta prima Lectione, ordinantur Ostiarii. Post secundam Lectionem, Lectores. Post tertiam Lectionem, Exorcistae. Post quartam, Acolythi." — Tit. *De Ordinibus Conferendis.*

13 "Si ordinationes fiant in Sabbato ante Dominicam de Passione, quia unica tantum dicitur Lectio, Tonsurae debent fieri immediate post Introitum. Omnes minores Ordines post *Kyrie, eleison.*" — Tit. *De Ordinibus Conferendis.*

14 "Si vero Sabbato ordinationes fiunt, . . . et Pontifex facit Confessionem, et dicto *Kyrie, eleison,* pro Missa, ordinat ad primam Tonsuram. Tum dicit, *Gloria in excelsis Deo,* etc. quo dicto, ordinat ad quatuor minores ordines." — Tit. *De Ordinibus Conferendis.*

> the general ordinations mentioned in paragraphs 2 and 3 of the same canon are performed, without doubt first tonsure and minor orders may also be conferred, although there be no ordination to sacred orders."[15]

It is clearly stated by the Sacred Congregation that the Minor Orders may be conferred on the Saturdays mentioned in paragraph two of canon 1006, when general ordinations are held, even though there be no ordination to Sacred Orders. It follows, then, that if it is only a particular ordination to Minor Orders, and these days are not of double rite, then these Saturdays will not, in this case, be proper days for an ordination to Minor Orders. Therefore, canon 1006, § 4, is not to be understood as giving the exclusive times for the conferring of Minors Orders, nor as prohibiting the conferral of Minor Orders on the solemn days of ordination.[16] Hence, Minor Orders may be given on the Ember Saturdays, the Saturday before Passion Sunday, and Holy Saturday, when a general ordination is held, even though Sacred Orders are not conferred.

Finally, the third enactment of the present law on the time for the conferring of Minor Orders is that the ceremony be performed only in the morning.[17] Thus, Minor Orders may be given at any hour before noon.[18] Augustine was of the opinion that *mane* includes the whole time during which it is permitted to say Mass, i.e., a Mass which is begun as early as one hour before dawn or as late as one hour after noon.[19] Romani even states that the Minor Orders could be conferred at midnight Mass of Christmas, even outside of Mass, as the law does not demand that the ordinations to Minor Orders take place during Mass.[20] But he also notes that Minor Orders cannot be conferred during a Mass which is celebrated in the evening,[21] or in the afternoon.

15 II, 250. [Editor's note] "The question to which this was a reply is not available. The reply was communicated to the *Canon Law Digest* for publication, through the kindness of the Most Reverend Apostolic Delegate to the United States."

16 Vermeersh, *Periodica,* XXII (1933), 136*-137*.

17 Can. 1006, § 4; *Pontificale Romanum,* Tit. *De Ordinibus Conferendis.*

18 Romani, *Institutiones Juris Canonici,* II, Pars I, n. 588.

19 *Commentary,* IV, 535; Can. 821.

20 *Institutiones Juris Canonici,* II, Pars I, n. 588.

21 *Loc. cit.*

The Code does not demand that the Minor Orders be conferred during Mass, and so a bishop could give them outside the celebration of Mass, but only in the morning. The Pontifical has the same regulation.[22]

In summary, the law regarding the time for the conferral of Minor Orders is that when general ordinations are held, they may be conferred on the Ember Saturdays, on the Saturday before Passion Sunday, and on Holy Saturday; or they also may be conferred on any Sunday or on any feast of double rite, but only in the morning.

Article 2. The time for re-ordination

> Canon 1007. — Quoties ordinatio iteranda sit vel aliquis ritus supplendus, sive absolute sive sub conditione, id fieri potest etiam extra tempora ac secreto.

The possibility of performing an ordination ceremony in an invalid manner is always present. Realizing this, the legislator, has provided for the eventuality in which some Minor Order has been conferred either invalidly, or defectively. The law regarding the time for re-ordination is most flexible, for it permits a re-ordination *extra-tempora.* This expression is interpreted by all to include any day of the year, even ferial days.[23] Thus, a re-ordination to Minor Orders, whether absolute or conditional, may take place on any day within the year, but again only in the morning.

When a re-ordination is held, it is permissible that on the same day, even *extra tempora,* many candidates for re-ordination may be ordained, and both the Major and Minor, may be conferred. Other candidates who are to receive Minor Orders for the first time, however, may not be ordained at the re-ordination if it takes place *extra tempora.*[24]

22 Tit. *De Ordinibus Conferendis.*

23 Augustine, *Commentary,* IV, 536; Bouscaren-Ellis, *Canon Law,* p. 392; Cappello, *De Ordine,* n. 565,4; Coronata, *De Sacramentis,* II, n. 241; Regatillo, *Ius Sacramentarium,* n. 995.

24 Aertnys-Damen, *Theologia Moralis,* II, n. 567; St. Alphonsus, *Theologia Moralis,* Lib. VI, n. 759; *supra,* p. 69.

ARTICLE 3. CUSTOMS CONTRARY TO THE TIME FOR ORDINATION TO MINOR ORDERS

Canon 1006, § 5. — Reprobatur consuetudo contra ordinationum tempora praecedentibus paragraphis praescripta; . . .

Despite the fact that ordinations to Minor Orders may be performed on so many days during the year, still it is possible that a custom contrary to the prescriptions of law regarding the time for conferring Minor Orders could have arisen. If such a custom did arise, or still exists, it must be abandoned, for the present law reprobates all contrary custom,[25] and a reprobated custom, even if centenary or immemorial, may not be allowed to continue, nor may it rise again in the future.[26] In fact, a new custom contrary to this law may not be introduced in the future, for a reprobated custom never obtains the consent of an ecclesiastical superior.[27]

Coronata observes that the Sacred Congregation of the Council on March 16 and April 13, 1720, declared that the custom of conferring Minor Orders on the Friday before the Ember Saturdays could be tolerated, but that it was expedient for the bishop to conform to the *Pontificale Romanum*.[28] In view of the present reprobation, this custom, if it still exists in some place, can no longer be permitted, a fact which Coronata fails to note.

It is to be observed that the reprobation of custom does not affect privileges, even if they be contrary to the Code, provided they were granted by the Apostolic See, were still in use, and were not revoked by the Code or before the Code.[29] Any privilege granted after the Code retains its value.

25 Can. 1006, § 5.

26 Can. 5.

27 Cann. 25, 27.

28 *De Sacramentis,* II, n. 238; *Supra,* p. 32.

29 Can. 4.

ARTICLE 4. THE TIME FOR INTERRITUAL ORDINATIONS

Canon 1006, § 5. — "... quae servanda quoque sunt, cum Episcopus latini ritus ordinat ex apostolico indulto clericum ritus orientalis aut contra."

When by apostolic indult a cleric of the Latin rite receives Minor Orders from the bishop of an Oriental rite, or a cleric of an Oriental rite receives Minor Orders from a bishop of the Latin rite, the Code directs that the norms established in canon 1006, § 4, regarding the time for the conferring of these Orders are to be followed.[30] This definitely marks an instance when the Orientals are bound to follow the Code.[31]

ARTICLE 5. DISPENSATIONS FROM THE LAW ON THE TIME FOR ORDINATIONS TO MINOR ORDERS

It hardly seems possible that it should become necessary to seek a dispensation from the law on the time for the conferring of Minor Orders, since the law permits such ordinations on a large number of days during the year. When, however, it happens that such a dispensation still is needed, it must be sought from the Holy See, and, more precisely, from the Sacred Congregation of the Sacraments. It is this Congregation which is competent in matters relating to the discipline of the sacraments.[32] A bishop could invoke canon 81 in an urgent case, since the Holy See is accustomed to dispense in this matter; but such a contingency would indeed be most rare. Even in this case, the bishop must first make use of the means of communication which the Apostolic Delegate has with the Holy See.[33]

SECTION B. THE PLACE FOR THE CONFERRING OF THE MINOR ORDERS

ARTICLE 1. THE PROPER TERRITORY

Canon 1008. — Episcopus extra propium territorium, sine Ordinarii loci licentia, nequit ordines conferre, in

30 Can. 1006, § 5.

31 Can. 1.

32 Can. 249.

33 *AAS*, XXXIX (1947), 374; *Canon Law Digest, Supplement Through 1948*, p. 15.

quorum collatione pontificalia exercentur, salvo praescripto can. 239, § 1, n. 15.

As was the case with the Major Orders, so in connection with the Minor Orders, two facts must be considered in determining the proper place for their conferral: first, the proper territory; and second, the place within the proper territory. The present article will treat of the former and the following article will deal with the latter.[34]

The Code repeats the previous legislation when it states that a bishop outside his own territory may not ordain to those Orders whose conferral involves the use of the pontificals, unless he has obtained the permission of the local ordinary of the place in which he wants to ordain, with any and all privileges in this matter as granted to Cardinals remaining intact. Consequently, whenever a bishop in conferring Minor Orders uses the pontificals (which in law include both the crozier and the mitre),[35] he is restricted to his own territory. In other words, the proper territory for this type of ordination is the bishop's own territory, unless he ordains in another territory with the permission of that local ordinary.

The one who grants the permission is the local ordinary of the diocese in which the ordination is to be held. Hence, any of those who come under the name "local ordinary" in law[36] may give an outside bishop, who wants to use the pontificals, permission to confer minor orders. The vicar general, however, must not use his power contrary to the mind and will of his bishop.[37]

The Roman Pontifical indicates that a bishop may confer Minor Orders outside of Mass, and that when he does so he need wear only

[34] *Infra,* p. 96.

[35] Can. 337, § 2; Augustine, *Commentary,* IV, 544; Beste, *Introductio in Codicem,* p. 547.

[36] Can. 198, § 1 — "In iure nomine *Ordinarii* intelliguntur, nisi quis expresse excipiatur, praeter Romanum Pontificem, pro suo quisque territorio Episcopus residentialis, Abbas vel Praelatus *nullius* eorumque Vicarius Generalis, Administrator, Vicarius et Praefectus Apostolicus, itemque ii qui praedictis deficientibus interim ex iuris praescripto aut ex probatis constitutionibus succedunt in regimine,..."

[37] Can. 369, § 2. "Caveat ne suis potestantibus utatur contra mentem et voluntatem sui Episcopi ..."

a stole over his rochet, and the simple mitre.[38] In this instance the bishop is conferring Minor Orders without the "pontificals," which in law includes both the crozier and the mitre.[39] Since the Minor Orders may be given without the use of the pontificals, a bishop may indeed ordain to Minor Orders outside his own territory without seeking the permission of the local ordinary in whose territory he ordains, but the bishop may confer Minor Orders only on his own subjects.[40] Thus, at least for his own subjects, the bishop when he ordains without pontificals may confer Minor Orders in any territory, even without the permission of the local ordinary.

The Code grants to vicars and prefects apostolic, even when they do not have the episcopal character, the power to give the Minor Orders, but only within some closely indicated limitations.[41] The same grant is also made to abbots and prelates *nullius* if they do not have the episcopal character.[42] These prelates, however, can ordain both their own subjects and others who present the proper dimissorial letters, but only in their own territory and during their tenure of office. Any ordination held by them beyond these limits is null and void.[43] This is one case in which the place of ordination affects the

38 "Quando autem Pontifex extra Missarum solemnia est promoturus aliquos ad primam Tonsuram, vel ad quatuor minores Ordines, sufficit quod habeat stolam supra rochettum, vel supra superpelliceum (si sit Regularis) et mitram simplicem." — Tit. *De Ordinibus Conferendis; De Minoribus Ordinibus*. Cf. *supra*, p. 74, footnote, n. 53.

39 Can. 337, § 2.

40 Beste, *Introductio in Codicem*, p. 547; Cappello, *De Ordine*, n. 568,1; *Summa*, II, n. 290, 1; Coronata, *De Sacramentis*, II, n. 242; Regatillo, *Ius Sacramentarium*, n. 997.

41 Can. 294, § 2. — "Etiam ii qui charactere episkopali carent, possunt, intra sui teritorii fines ac perdurante munere,... ordines minores conferre ad norman can. ...957, § 2."

42 Can. 323, § 2. "Si charactere episcopali non siit ornatus et benedictionem, si eam recipere debet, receperit, praeter alia munera quae in can. 294, § 2, describuntur, potest quoque ecclesias et altaria immobilia consecrare."

43 Can. 957, § 2. "Si episcopali charactere careant, possunt nihilominus in proprio territorio et durante tantum munere, conferre primam tonsuram et ordines minores tum propriis subditis saecularibus ad norman can. 956, tum aliis qui litteras dimissorias iure requisitas exhibeant; ordinatio extra hos fines ab eisdem peracta irrita est."

validity, and is an exception to the general rule. Therefore, when a vicar or a prefect apostolic, or an abbot or a prelate *nullius,* who is not a bishop confers Minor Orders, the proper territory is the confines of his own jurisdiction, and outside of it he acts invalidly.

Canon 1008 contains an exception in favor of cardinals. A cardinal by privilege is allowed to perform the functions which require the exercise of the pontificals in all churches outside of Rome, and in any cathedral, but in this event he must first notify the ordinary.[44] Hence, a cardinal may confer Minor Orders in any territory, whether or not he uses pontificals, and he does not need the permission of the local ordinary to do so. Augustine observed that the suburbicarian cardinal bishops are not allowed to confer orders in their private chapels in Rome without the permission of the Cardinal Vicar, according to the previously mentioned constitution of Benedict XIV.[45]

ARTICLE 2. THE PLACE WITHIN THE PROPER TERRITORY

> Canon 1009, § 3. — "...ordines minores conferri possunt etiam in privatis oratoriis."

The further question regarding the proper place within the proper territory for the conferring of Minor Orders is treated in canon 1009, § 3. With reference to the Minor Orders, no distinction is made in this canon between a general and a particular ordination. The canon simply states that the Minor Orders may be conferred also in private oratories. In law a private oratory is a place devoted to divine worship and erected in a private house for the benefit of some family or of a private person.[46] These chapels erected by families or by private persons in cemeteries for the burial of their own people are private oratories.[47] Any private oratory, then, is a

[44] Can. 239, § 1, n. 15; Augustine, *Commentary,* IV, 544-545; Blat, *Commentarium,* III, Pars I, n. 390; Regatillo, *Ius Sacramentarium,* n. 997.

[45] *Op. cit.,* IV, 545; *supra,* p. 45.

[46] Can. 1188, § 2, n. 3. "Est vero oratorium *Privatum* seu *domesticum,* si in privatis edibus in commodum alicuius tantum familiae vel personae privatae erectum sit."

[47] Can. 1190. — "Aediculae in coemeterio a familiis seu personis privatis ad suam sepulturam erectae, sunt oratoria privata."

proper place for the conferring of Minor Orders. Since the canon uses the word *"etiam,"* it seems obvious that the legislation is merely indicating the least important place which could serve as a proper place for the conferring of Minor Orders. Thus, Minor Orders may, *a fortiori,* be conferred also in places which are higher in rank, such as a semi-public oratory, a public oratory, or a church.[48] It may be noted that the bishop does not need a canonical reason or a cause for selecting one of these places in order to ordain candidates to the Minor Orders.[49]

Even when a bishop outside his own diocese ordains his own subjects to Minor Orders without using the pontificals, he must use at least a private oratory for the ceremony.

The Roman Pontifical contains the direction that Minor Orders may be given anywhere,[50] which before the Code meant any decent and fitting place, even though it was not of a sacred character.[51] Since the Code now demands at least a private oratory, it appears that on this point there is a change in the law, and that accordingly the prescription of the Pontifical cannot any longer be followed. Vermeersch-Creusen discuss canon 1009, § 3, and the norm of the Pontifical, but only in relation to tonsure. They state that, since the Pontifical allows tonsure to be conferred in any place, a light cause or reason will furnish a sufficient excuse from the observance of this prescription of the Code.[52] Since the Code treats tonsure and the Minor Orders together, it appears that the same solution may be applied to the Minor Orders. In other words, inasmuch as the Pontifical has *"ubicumque,"* any light cause will excuse from the observance of the prescription of the Code. Coronata says that, in reliance on the Pontifical, it is doctrinally admissable for ordinations to Minor Orders to be held in any decent and fitting place, even

48 Coronata, *De Sacramentis,* II, n. 245.

49 Cappello, *De Ordine,* n. 568,3; Regatillo, *Ius Sacramentarium,* n. 997,b.

50 "Minores vero Ordines possunt dari . . . ubicumque . . ." — Tit. *De Ordinibus Conferendis.*

51 Gasparri, *De Sacra Ordinatione,* I, n. 91; Many, *Praelectiones,* n. 100, *supra,* p. 59.

52 *Epitome Iuris Canoici,* II, n. 270, 2.

though it has not been set aside for divine worship.[53] However, it seems that the interpretation of Vermeersch-Creusen is closer to canonical exactness, and hence a bishop needs at least a light cause in order to confer Minor Orders in a place other than one set aside for divine worship, that is, in at least a private oratory.

Finally, it may be noted that any place which is under a general or a particular local interdict is not a proper place for the conferring of Minor Orders.[54]

ARTICLE 3. THE PROPER PLACE FOR CONFERRING MINOR ORDERS ON RELIGIOUS

The norms which have been mentioned in the foregoing articles also bind religious. There is, however, an added consideration in the matter of establishing the proper place of ordination to Minor Orders for religious, and that is: In which diocese are they to be ordained? The general rule, exclusive of any privilege or indult which a particular institute may have, calls for a religious to be ordained in that diocese in which is located the religious house to which the candidate for Orders belongs. This norm is drawn from the canon which determines the bishop to whom a religious superior must send the dimissorial letters.[55] Usually a religious superior is not empowered to give Minor Orders, and so must of necessity send his subjects to some bishop (or vicar or prefect apostolic, or abbot or prelate *nullius*), who can confer Minor Orders. Canon 965 determines the bishop to whom the superior must send the dimissorials, and consequently it also determines the diocese where the religious is to receive Minor Orders, namely, the diocese in which the religious house is situated.

Special circumstances are mentioned in canon 966, § 1, which permits a religious to receive the Minor Orders in another diocese. This holds true when the bishop of the place where the religious house is located gives his permission; or when the bishop is of a different rite; or when the bishop is absent; or when he will not hold ordinations at the next legitimate time according to canon 1006, § 2;

[53] *De Sacramentis,* II, n. 245.

[54] Can. 2270, § 1. — "Interdictum locale sive generale sive particulare ... prohibet in loco quodlibet divinum officium vel sacrum ritum ..."

[55] Can. 965; *supra,* p. 84.

or when the administrator of a vacant diocese has not the episcopal character. In all these cases a religious may, when the proper dimissorials have been furnished, receive Minor Orders in some diocese other than the one in which his house is located. An authentic notification that such a reason is really present must be sent to the ordaining bishop by the curia of the bishop who ordinarily would be the proper bishop.[56] Furthermore, religious superiors are warned not to deprive by fraud the proper diocesan bishop of his right to ordain the candidates in question,[57] and should they presume to violate the prescriptions of canons 965-967, they would incur *ipso facto* a suspension from the celebration of Mass for a month.[58]

It may be noted that, if proper dimissorial letters have been sent to the bishop, then the bishop without pontificals could even in places outside his diocese, confer the Minor Orders on the religious who have houses in his diocese.[59]

The members of societies of the common life[60] in the matter of receiving Orders follow the laws which regulate the secular clergy, unless they have privileges or indults to the contrary.[61] Accordingly they are to be ordained in the territory of their proper bishop, who is determined according to canon 956. With proper dimissorial letters, their own oratories would be a proper place for conferring the Minor Orders, if the local bishop should chose to use this place. Usually they receive Minor Orders in the place wherein the secular clergy receives them.

The Code mentions another who, besides bishops, vicars and prefects apostolic, abbots and prelates *nullius,* has the power to confer

[56] Can. 966, § 2; *supra,* p. 85.

[57] Can. 967; *supra,* p. 85.

[58] Can. 2410; *supra,* pp. 85-86.

[59] *Supra,* p. 95.

[60] Can. 673, § 1. — "Societas sive virorum sive mulierum, in qua sodales vivendi rationem religiosorum imitantur in communi degentes sub regimine Superiorum secundum probatas constitutiones, sed tribus consuetis votis publicis non obstringuntur, non est proprie religio, nec eius sodales nomine religiosorum proprie designantur."

[61] Can. 678. — "In iis quae ad studiorum rationem et ad suscipiendos ordines pertinent, sodales iisdem legibus tenentur ac saeculares clerici, salvis peculiaribus praescriptionibus a Sancta Sede datis."

Minor Orders, and that is an abbot *de regimine.* In this instance certain conditions must be fulfilled in order that such an abbot *de regimine*—i.e., one actually holding office with ordinary jurisdiction over his subjects[62]—may validly confer Minor Orders; namely, that along with being an abbot *de regimine* he be a priest; that he have legitimately received the abbatial blessing, and that the candidate for Orders be his subject by at least simple profession.[63] Thus, a merely titular abbot, an abbot primate, or an abbot who is president of a monastic congregation, is not strictly speaking an abbot *de regimine.* Only with a special privilege may a titular abbot, an abbot primate, or any abbot who is president of a monastic congregation, confer Minor Orders.[64] Therefore, the proper place of ordination to Minor Orders for those religious who by at least simple profession are the subjects of an abbot *de regimine* is the monastery over which the abbot rules; but even in this case at least a private oratory must be used.

A further question arises: May an abbot *de regimine,* when he is a priest who has legitimately received the abbatial blessing, in a place outside of his monastery confer Minor Orders on candidates who are his subjects by at least simple profession? This case is not covered by canon 964, n. 1. There are two aspects to be considered. First, if the abbot *de regimine* outside of his monastery should confer Minor Orders on such as are his subjects by at least simple profession, would he ordain validly? Since the Code does not expressly or equivalently declare such an act invalid, it seems one may conclude that such an ordination would be valid, for the only invalidating laws are those which expressly or equivalently declare an act null and void, or a person incapacitated or disqualified.[65] Secondly, if

[62] Bouscaren-Ellis, *Canon Law,* p. 363.

[63] Can. 964, n.1, "Abbas regularis de regimine, etsi sine territorio *nullius,* potest conferre primam tonsuram et ordines minores, dummodo promovendus sit ipsi subditus vi professionis saltem simplicis, ipse vero sit presbyter et benedictionem abbatialem legitime acceperit. Extra hos fines, ordinatio, ab eodem collata, revocato quolibet contrario privilegio, est irrita, nisi ordinans charactere episcopali polleat."

[64] Coronata, *De Sacramentis,* II, n. 41.

[65] Can. 11 — "Irritantes aut inhabilitantes eae tantum leges habendae sunt, quibus aut actum esse nullum aut inhabilem esse personam expresse vel aequivalenter statuitur."

the abbot *de regimine* outside of his monastery confers Minor Orders on candidates who are his subjects by at least simple profession, would he ordain lawfully? Since the Code puts no restriction with regard to place on the abbot *de regimine,* it seems that the rules which regulate the proper place for the conferring of Minor Orders by a bishop may be applied here also. Thus, if the abbot *de regimine,* with the use of the pontificals (both the crozier and the mitre) wants to confer Minor Orders outside of his monastery, then he needs the permission of the local ordinary of the diocese where the ceremony is to be held. If, however, the abbot *de regimine* does not use the pontificals, then he may anywhere lawfully confer Minor Orders on candidates who are his subjects by at least simple profession, and he may do this without obtaining the permission of the local ordinary.[66] Of course, in these circumstances, the abbot *de regimine* must still use at least a private oratory for the ceremony.

In summary, the proper territory for the conferring of Minor Orders on religious is, in general, the diocese in which is situated the religious house to which the religious candidates for Orders belongs. For regulars subject to an abbot *de regimine,* the proper place for receiving Minor Orders is the monastery over which the abbot *de regimine* rules and to which the religious belongs; the same abbot may, however, when he confers Minor Orders on candidates who are his subjects by at least simple profession, do so outside the monastery with the permission of the local ordinary if he uses the pontificals, or even without this permission if he does not use the pontificals.

66 *Supra,* pp. 94-95.

CHAPTER VII
TONSURE

Section A. The Time for Conferring Tonsure

> Canon 1006, § 4. — "Prima tonsura quolibet die et hora conferri potest . . ."

The Code in regulating the time for the conferring of tonsure merely repeats the law which has existed for centuries. Thus, any day within the year (even such a day as Good Friday) and any hour of the day may be selected as a proper time for the conferring of tonsure. This norm is also stated in the Roman Pontifical.[1]

Inasmuch as the time is all-inclusive, their cannot be any question of a contrary custom, or any discussion of a time for re-ordination, or any problem in the seeking of a dispensation. This norm also serves for an inter-ritual ordination, and is to be followed by an Oriental bishop when he tonsures a person of the Latin rite, or when a Latin bishop tonsures a person of an Oriental rite by apostolic indult.[2]

Section B. The Place for Conferring Tonsure

Article 1. The Proper Territory for Conferring Tonsure

> Canon 1008. — "Episcopus extra proprium territorium, sine Ordinarii loci licentia, nequit ordines conferre, in quorum collatione pontificalia exercentur, salvo praescripto can. 239, § 1, n. 15."

As with the Minor Orders, so also with the tonsure there is a twofold question to be considered: first, the proper territory; and second, the place within the proper territory. The first will be

[1] Tit. *De Ordinibus Conferendis; De Clerico faciendo.*

[2] Can. 1006, § 5.

treated in this article, and the second in the following article.[3]

It may be stated as a general principle that the rules which govern the conferring of tonsure are the same as those which control the conferring of Minor Orders.[4] These norms, however, will receive mention only in summary form in this article, and without a repetition of any of the discussions set forth regarding the element of place in the chapter on Minor Orders.

Tonsure may be conferred with or without the use of the pontificals.[5] When the bishop uses the pontificals, then by canon 1008 he is restricted to the confines of his own territory; but, should he desire to confer tonsure outside his territory and with the use of pontificals (the crozier and the mitre),[6] he must obtain the permission of the ordinary of the place where this ordination is to be held. Anyone who in law comes under the title of local ordinary is the proper authority of the diocese to grant the permission.[7] The vicar general, however, should act in accord with the mind and the will of his bishop.[8]

On the other hand, if the bishop does not use the pontificals, then he may tonsure his own subjects even outside his diocese; and in this case he does not need the permission of the ordinary of the place where the ordination takes place.

Vicars and prefects apostolic, prelates and abbots *nullius,* also when they lack the episcopal character, have from the Code power to confer tonsure,[9] but only while they have tenure of office, and only within their own territory.[10] Hence, they could not validly tonsure even their own subjects outside their own territory. This is one case when the place has some effect on the validity of an ordination.

3 *Infra,* p. 104.

4 *Supra,* pp. 93-96.

5 "Quando autem Pontifex extra Missarum solemnia est promoturus aliquos ad primam Tonsuram,... sufficit quod habeat stolam supra rochettum, vel supra superpelliceum (si sit Regularis) et mitram simplicem." — *Pontificale Romanum,* Tit. *De Ordinibus Conferendis; De Clerico faciendo.*

6 Can. 337, § 2.

7 Can. 198.

8 Can. 369, § 2.

9 Cans. 294, § 2; 323.

10 Can. 957, § 2.

Thus, when these prelates ordain, their own proper territory marks off the limits of their capacity for conferring Orders. They may, however, validly ordain subjects of other bishops, when the candidates come to them with the proper dimissorial letters.[11]

Cardinals may with the use of the pontificals confer tonsure in any territory, for by privilege they may in any church outside of Rome perform rites which demand the exercise of the pontificals. Only when a cardinal desires to use a cathedral is he expected previously to inform the ordinary.[12] The suburbicarian cardinal bishops are not permitted to confer tonsure in their private chapels in Rome without the permission of the Cardinal Vicar.[13]

Article 2. The Place Within the Proper Territory

> Canon 1009, § 3. — "Prima tonsura . . . conferri potest etiam in privatis oratoriis."

The Code demands at least a private oratory[14] as a proper place for conferring tonsure. Hence, *a fortiori*, any more important place will also serve the same purpose. Such places are the semi-public or public oratories, and also the churches. This rule must likewise be followed whenever a bishop without the use of the pontificals confers tonsure on his subjects outside his diocese. Any place which is under a general or a particular local interdict ceases to be a lawful place for the conferring of tonsure.[15]

The Roman Pontifical directs that tonsure may be given in "any place,"[16] which phrase was interpreted in the pre-Code law to mean

[11] Can. 957, § 2.

[12] Can. 239, § 1, n. 15.

[13] Augustine, *Commentary*, IV, 545; *supra*, p. 96.

[14] Can. 1188, § 2, n. 3.

[15] Can. 2270. In § 2 *"collatio ordinum"* is to be understood according to the meaning of canon 950. Hence, the conferring of tonsure is included under the prohibition of can. 2270, since neither the nature of the matter in question nor the context of the canon itself calls for an exclusion with reference to tonsure.

[16] "Clericatus, seu prima Tonsura, quocumque die, hora, et loco conferri potest." — Tit. *De Ordinibus Conferendis.*

Clericus fieri potest etiam extra Missarum solemnia quocumque die, hora, et loco." — Tit. *De Clerico faciendo.*

any decent and fitting place, even though it had not been set aside for divine worship.[17] The regulation in the Code requires at least a private oratory.[18] Accordingly the Code has made a change in the law, and this innovation needs to be followed. Vermeersch-Creusen, who dealt very expressly with this question, stated that the Code is to be followed, but that in view of the prescription of the Pontifical a light cause or reason will excuse one from observing the regulation of the Code.[19] Coronata contends that, in line with the ruling contained in the Pontifical, it is doctrinally feasible for the Minor Orders to be conferred in any place, provided it be a decent and fitting place, even though it has not been set aside for divine worship.[20] While indeed he is speaking of the Minor Orders, yet the argument which he uses to support his opinion is, *a fortiori*, applicable to the conferring of tonsure. It seems, however, that the interpretation of Vermeersch-Creusen is more in conformity with canonical reasoning, and so for the conferring of tonsure some light reason is required for the use of a decent and fitting place which is not set aside for divine worship.

Article 3. The Proper Place for Conferring Tonsure on Religious

With regard to the proper place for the receiving of tonsure, religious are bound by the same rules that govern their reception of the Minor Orders. Therefore it is not necessary to repeat the discussion contained in article 2 of Chapter VI, but it will be sufficient to give a summary. As a general rule, the proper territory within which a religious is to receive tonsure is the place wherein is located the religious house to which he belongs.[21] Unless a contrary privilege of indult be in force, a religious may go to another territory only when the bishop gives his permission; or when the bishop is of a different rite; or when the bishop is absent; or when the bishop will not hold ordinations at the next lawful time according to canon 1006,

[17] Gasparri, *De Sacra Ordinatione*, I, n. 91; Many, *Praelectiones*, n. 100; Pirhing, Lib. I, tit. XI, n. 76; Schmalzgrueber, Lib. I, tit. XI, n. 17.

[18] Vermeersch-Creusen, *Epitome Iuris Canonici*, II, n. 270, 2.

[19] *Loc. cit.*

[20] *De Sacramentis*, II, n. 245.

[21] Can. 965.

§ 2 (the Ember Saturdays, the Saturday before Passion Sunday, or Holy Saturday); or when the administrator of a vacant see is himself not a bishop, or is himself without the faculty of conferring tonsure.[22] Superiors cannot fraudulently deprive the diocesan bishop of his right to ordain the candidates in question,[23] and any who would do so would incur *ipso facto* a suspension from saying Mass for a month.[24]

An abbot *de regimine,* when he is a priest who has lawfully received the abbatial blessing, may within the confines of his monastery confer tonsure on candidates who are his subjects by at least simple profession.[25] Furthermore, he may validly and lawfully confer tonsure on these subjects outside of his monastery with the permission of the ordinary of the territory where the ceremony is held, if the abbot *de regimine* uses the pontificals (crozier and mitre); and he may do so even without such a permission if he does not use the pontificals.[26]

If someone is indeed subject to the abbot *de regimine,* but has not yet made his simple profession, then he is bound to receive tonsure from his proper bishop, who is to be determined according to canon 956. This latter rule also binds the members of a society of the common life.[27]

Religious, like the others, must receive tonsure in at least a private oratory, unless the existence of at least some light cause or reason permits the use of another decent and fitting place, even though it has not been set aside for divine worship.[28]

[22] Can. 966, § 1.

[23] Can. 967; cf. can. 950. — "Ii iure verba: *ordinare, ordo, ordinatio, Sacra ordinatio,* comprehendunt, praeter consecrationem episcopalem, ordines enumeratos in can. 949, et ipsam tonsuram, nisi aliud ex natura rei vel ex contextu verborum eruatur."

[24] Can. 2410.

[25] Can. 964, n. 1.

[26] Cf. *supra,* pp. 100-101.

[27] Cans. 673, 678.

[28] Can. 1009, § 3; *supra,* pp. 104-105.

CONCLUSIONS

1. It is the Sacred Consistorial Congregation that is competent to dispense from the observance of the canonical times for episcopal consecration. (p. 54)

2. The suppressed holy days of obligation are not legitimate times for holding ordinations to Sacred Orders, even when there is present a grave reason; but all the holy days of obligation for the universal Church are proper times for sacred ordinations under canon 1006, § 3. (pp. 64-65)

3. The diocesan consultors, even though they take the place of the cathedral chapter in the government of the diocese, are not under obligation to be present at ordinations which are held in the cathedral. (pp. 79-80)

4. The oratory of a "religious house," which according to canon 1009, § 2, may for a just cause be a proper place for a particular ordination, is to be understood as including also the oratories of societies of the common life. (p. 83)

5. A light cause is sufficient for a bishop to confer Minor Orders and tonsure outside a private oratory in a decent and fitting place, even though the place has not been set aside for divine worship. (pp. 97-98; 105)

6. An abbot *de regimine* may outside his monastery validly confer Minor Orders and tonsure on candidates who are his subjects by at least simple profession; and lawfully with the permission of the ordinary of the place where the ceremony is to be held, if the abbot *de regimine* uses the pontificals (both the crozier and the mitre); and lawfully also without the permission of the local ordinary, if the abbot *de regimine* does not use the pontificals. (pp. 100-101; 106)
179)

BIBLIOGRAPHY

Sources

Acta Apostolicae Sedis, Commentarium Officiale, Romae, 1909-1929; Civitate Vaticana, 1929—

Acta Sanctae Sedis, 41 vols., Romae, 1865-1908.

Benedicti XIV Bullarium, 3 vols. in 4, Prati, 1845-1847.

Bouscaren, T. Lincoln, *The Canon Law Digest,* 2 vols, and Supplement through 1948, Milwaukee, Wis.: The Bruce Publishing Co., 1934-1943-1949.

Bruns, H., *Canones Apostolorum et Conciliorum Saeculorum IV-VII,* 2 vols., Berolini, 1839.

Bullarum Diplomatum et Privilegiorum Sanctorum Pontificum Taurinensis Editio, 24 vols. et Appendix, Augustae Taurinorum, 1857-1872.

Codicis Iuris Canonici Fontes, cura Emi Petri Card. Gasparri editi, 9 vols., Romae (postea Civitate Vaticana): Typis Polyglottis Vaticanis, 1923-1939. (Vols. VII-IX, ed. cura et studio Emi Iustiniani Card. Serédi.)

Collectanea S. Congregationis de Propaganda Fide, 2 vols., Romae: Typographia Polyglotta S.C. de Propaganda Fide, 1907.

Corpus Iuris Canonici, ed. Lipsiensis secunda, post Aemilii Richteri curas ... instruxit Aemilius Friedberg, 2 vols., Lipsiae, 1879-1881.

Decreta Authentica Congregationis Sacrorum Rituum, 5 vols. et 2 appendices, Romae: Ex Typographia Polyglotta, 1898-1927.

Decretles D. Gregorii Papae IX suae integritati una cum glossis restitutae, Romae, 1582.

Decretum Gratiani, emendatum et notationibus illustratum una cum glossis Gregorii XIII Pont. Max. iussu editum, 2 vols., Romae, 1582.

Denzinger, Heinrich — Bannwart, Clemens — Umberg, Johannes, *Enchiridion Symbolorum, Definitionum, et Declarationum de Rebus Fidei et Morum,* 21.-23. ed., Friburgi Brisgoviae: Herder & Co., 1937.

Epistolae Romanorum Pontificium Genuinae et Quae ad Eos Scriptae Sunt, a S. Hilaro usque ad Pelagium II, ed. Andreas Thiel, Vol. I *A S. Hilaro usque ad S. Hormisdam,* Brunsbergae, 1868.

Hinschius, Paulus, *Decretales Pseudo-Isidorianae et Capitulae Angilramni,* Lipsiae, 1863.

Jaffé, Philippus, *Regesta Pontificum Romanorum ab condita Ecclesia ad annum post Christum natum MCXCVIII,* ed. 2 correctam et auctam Gulielmi Wattenbach curaverunt S. Loewenfeld, F. Kaltenbrunner, P. Ewald, 2 vols., Lipsiae, 1885-1888.

Labbeus, P., Cossartius, G., *Sacrosancta Concilia,* 17 vols. in 18, Parisiis, 1671-1672.

Les Registres de Grégoire IX, ed. Lucien Auvray, 3 vols., Paris, 1896-1907.

Magnum Bullarium Romanum, 19 vols. in 18, Luxemburgi, 1727-1754.

Mansi, J. D., *Sacrorum Conciliorum Nova et Amplissima Collectio,* 53 vols. in 60, Parisiis, 1901-1927.

Migne, J. P., *Patrologiae Cursus Completus, Series Graeca,* 161 vols., Parisiis, 1857-1866.

———, *Patrologiae Cursus Completus, Series Latina,* 221 vols., Parisiis, 1844-1855.

Missale Romanum ex decreto Sacrosancti Concilii Tridentini restitutum, S. Pii V Potificis Maximi iussu editum, aliorum Pontificum cura recognitum, a Pio X reformatum et Benedicti XV auctoritate vulgatum, editio II juxta typicam vaticanam, amplificata I, New York: Benziger Brothers, Inc., 1942.

Monumenta Germaniae Historica, Legum Sectio III, *Concilia,* 3 vols., edd. F. Maassen, A. Werminghoff, H. Bastgen, Hannoverae, 1893-1924.

Octoginta quinque Regulae, seu Canones Apostolorum, Parisiis, 1558.

Pallottini, Salvator, *Collectio omnium conclusionum et resolutionum quae in causis propositis apud Sacram Congregationem Cardinalium S. Concilii Tridentini Interpretum prodierunt ab ius institutione anno MDLXIV ad annum MDCCCLX, distinctis titulis alphabetico ordine per materias digesta,* 17 vols., Romae, 1868-1893.

Potthast, Augustus, *Regesta Pontificum Romanorum inde ab anno post Christum natum* 1198 *ad annum* 1304, 2 vols., Berolini, 1874-1875.

Sacramentarium Leonianum, ed. Rev. Charles Feltoe, Cambridge: University Press, 1896.

Schroeder, H. J., *Canons and Decrees of the Council of Trent,* St. Louis: B. Herder, 1941.

Thesaurus Resolutionum Sacrae Congregationis Concilii, 167 vols., Urbini-Romae, 1718-1908.

Reference Works

Abbo, John — Hannan, Jerome, *The Sacred Canons, A Concise Presentation of the Current Disciplinary Norms of the Church,* 2 vols., St. Louis: B. Herder Book Co., 1952.

Aertnys, J. — Damen, C., *Theologia Moralis,* 16. ed., 2 vols., Taurini: Marietti, 1950.

Andrieu, Michel, *Le Pontifical Romain au Moyen Age,* Vols. 86-87 in *Studi e Testi,* Vatican City: Vatican Press, 1938-1940.

Augustine, Charles, *A Commentary on the New Code of Canon Law,* 8 vols., Vol. IV, 3. ed., St. Louis: Herder & Co., 1925.

Barbosa, A., *De Officio et Potestate Episcopi,* 2 vols., Lugduni, 1656.

Benedictus XIV, *Opera Omnia in Unum Corpus Collecta,* 15 vols. in 7, Tom. Undecimus, *De Synodo Dioecesana,* Venetiis, 1788.

Beste, Udalricus, O.S.B., *Introductio in Codicem,* 3. ed., Collegeville: St. John's Abbey Press, 1948.

Bingham, Joseph, *Antiquities of the Christian Church,* 2 vols., London, 1856.

Blat, Albertus, O.P., *Commentarium Textus Codicis Iuris Canonici,* 6 vols., Romae: Ex Typographia Pontificia in Instituto Pii X, 1919-1927.

Bouscaren, T. Lincoln, S.J. — Ellis, Adam, S.J., *Canon Law, A Text and Commentary,* Milwaukee: The Bruce Publishing Company, 1949.

Cappello, Felix, *Summa Iuris Canonici,* 3 vols., Romae: Apud Aedes Universitatis Gregorianae, Vol. I and II, 4. ed., 1945; Vol. III, 2. ed., 1940, Romae: Universitas Gregoriana.

———, *Tractatus Canonico-Moralis de Sacramentis,* 5 vols., Vol. IV, 2. ed., 1947, Torino: Marietti.

Catalani, Joseph, *Pontificale Romanum in tres partes distributum Clementis VIII ac Urbani VIII auctoritate recognitum nunc primum prolegomenis et commentariis illustratum,* 2. ed., 3 vols., Parisiis, 1850-1852.

Coronata, Matthaeus Conte a, *Institutiones Iuris Canonici, De Sacramentis Tractatus Canonicus,* 3 vols., Torino: Marietti, 1943-1946.

———, *Institutiones Iuris Canonici,* 5 vols., Vols. I, II, 2. ed., 1939; Vol. III, 2. ed., 1941; Vol. IV, 2. ed., 1945; Vol. V, 2. ed., 1947, Taurini: Marietti.

Crnica, Antonius, *Commentarium Theoretico-Practicum Codicis Iuris Canonici,* 2 vols., Sibenik: Typis Typographiae "Kačić", 1940-1941.

De Puniet, Pierre, *The Roman Pontifical, A History and Commentary,* translated by Mildred V. Harcourt, London: Longmans, Green & Co., 1932. Deusdedit, Kardinal, *Die Kanonessammlung,* neu herausgegeben von Victor Wolf von Glanvell, Paderborn, 1905, p. 184.

Deusdedit, Kardinal, *Die Kanonessammlung,* neu herausgegeben von Victor Wolf von Glanvell, Paderborn, 1905.

Duchesne, L., *Le Liber Pontificalis: Texte, Introduction, et Commentaire,* 2 vols., Paris, 1886-1892.

Fagnanus, P., *Commentaria in Quinque Libros Decretalium,* 5 vols. in 3, Venetiis, 1697.

Gasparri, P., *Tractatus Canonicus de Sacra Ordinations,* 2 vols., Parisiis, 1893.

Genicot, Eduardus — Salsmans, J., *Theologiae Moralis Institutiones,* 6. ed., 2 vols., Bruxellis, 1909.

Ghilardi, Joannes T., *Epitome Canonum Conciliorum tum Generalium tum Provincialium ab Apostolis usque ad annum MDCIX per Alphabeticum digesta,* 2 vols. in 1, Monteregali, 1870.

Giraldi, U., *Expositio Iuris Pontificii iuxta recentionem Ecclesiae disciplinam in duas partes distributa,* 3 vols. in 2, Romae, 1769.

Hallier, F., *De Sacris Electionibus et Ordinationibus ex antiquo et novo Ecclesiae Usu,* 3 vols., Romae, 1740.

Hostiensis, Cardinalis (Henricus de Segusio), *In Decretalium Libros Commentaria,* 5 vols. in 3, Venetiis, 1581.

Innocentius IV, *In V. Libros Decretalium Commentaria,* Venetiis, 1570.

Liguori, Alphonsus, St., *Theologia Moralis,* ed. nova cura L. Gaudé, 7 libri in 4 vols., Romae, 1905-1912.

Loomis, Louise R., *The Book of the Popes,* Records of Civilization: Sources and Studies, ed. James Shotwell, n. 3, New York: Columbia University Press, 1916.

Many, Seraphinus, *Praelectiones de Sacra Ordinatione,* Parisiis; Letouzey et Ané, 1905.

Naz, Raoul, *Traité de Droit Canonique,* 4 vols., Vol. II *Des Sacrements,* par Charles de Clercq, Paris: Letouzey et Ané, 1947.

Noldin, H., — Schmitt, A., *Summa Theologiae Moralis,* 3 vols., 26. ed., Oeniponte/Lipsiae: Sumtibus et Typis Feliciani Rauch, 1940.

Panormitanus, Abbas (Nicholaus de Tudeschis), *Commentaria in Quinque Libros Decretalium,* 5 vols. in 7, Venetiis, 1588.

Percival, H., *The Seven Ecumenical Councils of the Universal Church. Their Canons and Dogmatic Decrees together with the Canons of all the local Synods which have received Ecumenical Acceptance,* New York, 1901.

Pirhing, E., *Ius Canonicum in V Libros Decretalium,* 5 vols. in 4, Dilingae, 1674-1678.

Quasten, Johannes, *Monumenta Eucharistica et Liturgica Vetustissima,* Bonnae, 1935.

Regatillo, E., *Ius Sacramentarium,* 2. ed., Sal Terrae: Santander, 1949.

Reiffenstuel, A., *Ius Canonicum Universum,* 5 vols. in 7, Parisiis, 1864-1870.

Riganti, J. B., *Commentaria in Regulas, Constitutiones et Ordinationes Cancellariae Apostolicae,* 2 vols., Coloniae Allobrogum, 1751.

Romani, Silvio, *Institutiones Juris Canonici,* 2 vols. in 3, Romae: Editrice "Iustitia," 1941-1945.

Rufinus, *Summa Decretorum,* ed. Heinrich Singer, Paderborn, 1902.

Schmalzgrueber, F., *Ius Ecclesiasticum Universum,* 5 vols. in 12, Romae, 1843-1845.

Schroeder, H. J., *Disciplinary Decrees of the General Councils,* St. Louis: B. Herder, 1937.

Thaner, F., *Anselmi Episcopi Lucensis Collectio Canonum una cum Collectione Minore iussu Instituti Savignani,* Oeniponte, 1906.

Thomassinus, L., *Vetus et Nova Ecclesiae Disciplina circa Beneficia et Beneficiarios,* 3 vols., Parisiis, 1691.

Van Hove, A., *Commentarium Lovaniense in Codicem Iuris Canonici,* Vol. I Tom. I, *Prolegomena,* 2. ed., Mechliniae/Romae: H. Dessain, 1945.

Vermeersch, A. — Creusen, J., *Epitome Iuris Canonici,* 6. ed., 3 vols., Mechliniae/Romae: H. Dessain, 1937-1946.

Woywod, S. — Smith, C., *A Practical Commentary on the Code of Canon Law,* 2 vols., New York: Joseph F. Wagner, Inc., 1948.

Zonaras, J., *In Canones SS. Apostolorum et Sacrorum Conciliorum Commentaria,* Parisiis, 1618.

Articles

————, "Day for Conferring Sacred Orders," Cases and Studies, *The Ecclesiastical Review,* LXV (1921), 423-425.

Lardone, C., "Il tempo delle Sacre Ordinazione," *Perfice Munus,* I (1926), 240-241.

Pauwels, J., "In alterum responsum de Tempore Sacrae Ordinationis," *Periodica de Re Morali, Canonica, Liturgica,* XXV (1936), 207-208.

Roberti, F., "Comment on decree of the Code Commission," *Apollinaris,* IX (1936), 590-592.

Periodicals

American Ecclesiastical Review, The, American Ecclesiastical Review, Vols. I — XXXII, Philadelphia, 1889-1905; *The Ecclesiastical Review,* Philadelphia, 1905-1943; from 1944, *The American Ecclesiastical Review,* Washington, D.C., Vol. CX, 1944—

Apollinaris, Romae, 1928—

Jurist, The., Washington, D.C., 1941—

Perfice Munus, Torino, 1926—

Periodica de Re Morali, Canonica Liturgica, Brugis, 1927-1936; Romae, 1937—

ABBREVIATIONS

AAS—Acta Apostolicae Sedis.

AER—The American Ecclesiastical Review.

ASS—Acta Sanctae Sedis.

Bened. XIV Bull.—Benedicti XIV Bullarium.

Collectanea—Collectanea S. Congregationis de Propaganda Fide.

Decr. Auth.—Decreta Authentica Sacrorum Rituum Congregationis.

ER—The Ecclesiastical Review.

Fontes—Codicis Iuris Canonici Fontes.

JE—Jaffé, *Regesta Pontificum Romanorum* (edited by P. Ewald, for the years 590-882).

JK—Jaffé, *op. cit.* (edited by F. Kaltenbrunner, to the year 590).

JL—Jaffé, *op. cit.* (edited by S. Loewenfeld, for the years 882-1198).

Magnum Bull. Rom.—Magnum Bullarum Romanum.

Mansi—*Sacrorum Conciliorum Nova et Amplissima Collectio.*

MGH—Monumenta Germaniae Historica.

MPG—Migne, *Patrologia, Series Graeca.*

MPL—Migne, *Patrologia, Series Latina.*

S.C.C.—Sacra Congregatio Concilii.

S.C.S. Off.—Sacra Congregatio Sancti Officii.

S.R.C.—Sacrorum Rituum Congregatio.

Taurinensis Bullarum Editio—Bullarum Diplomatum et Privilegiorum Sanctorum Pontificum Taurinensis Editio.

Thesaurus—Thesaurus Resolutionum Sacrae Congregationis Concilii.

ALPHABETICAL INDEX

BIOGRAPHICAL NOTE

John Charles Reiss was born May 13, 1922, in Red Bank, New Jersey. He received his elementary education at St. James' Parochial School, and his secondary education at Red Bank Catholic High School. In the fall of 1939 he entered the undergraduate School of Arts and Sciences at The Catholic University of America. Two years later he transferred to the major seminary of the Immaculate Conception at Darlington, N. J. In 1946 he entered the School of Sacred Theology at The Catholic University, and in June, 1947, received the degree of Licentiate of Sacred Theology. The same year he also received from Seton Hall College, South Orange, N. J. —affiliated with the Immaculate Conception Seminary—the degree of Bachelor of Arts for work which he had completed while he was in the seminary. He was ordained to the priesthood on May 31, 1947, by His Excellency, William A. Griffin, Bishop of Trenton. For the next three years he served as parochial assistant in a number of parishes in the Diocese of Trenton. In October, 1950, he enrolled in the School of Canon Law at The Catholic University of America, and received the degree of Bachelor of Canon Law in June, 1951. In June, 1952, he received the degree of Licentiate of Canon Law.

CANON LAW STUDIES *

337. Bourque, Rev. John R., S.T.L., J.C.L., The judicial power of the Church — Canon 1553, § 1
338. Cornell, Rev. Charles E., A.B., S.T.B., J.C.L., The juridical status of heretics and schismatics in good faith
339. Fitzgerald, Rev. William Francis, A.B., S.T.L., J.C.L., The parish census and the *liber status animarum*
340. Kubik, Rev. Stanislaus J., S.T.D., J.C.L., Invalidity of dispensations according to canon 84, § 1
341. Nugent, Rev. John Gerard, C.M., J.C.L., Ordination in societies of the common life
342. Peterson, Rev. Casimir Melvyn, S.S., A.B., S.T.L., J.C.L., Spiritual care in diocesan seminaries
343. Reiss, Rev. John Charles, A.B., S.T.L., J.C.L., The time and place of sacred ordination
344. Sheehan, Rev. Joseph, J.C.L., The obligation of respect and obedience of clerics to their ordinary — Canon 127
345. Shekleton, Rev. Matthew M., O.S.M., J.C.L., Doctrinal interpretation of law
346. Viau, Rev. Roger, S.T.L., J.C.L., Doubt in Canon Law
347. Walsh, Rev. Donnell Anthony, A.B., J.C.L., The new law on secular institutes

* For a complete list of the available numbers of this series apply to The Catholic University of America Press, 620 Michigan Avenue, N.E., Washington (17), D.C.

www.ingramcontent.com/pod-product-compliance
Lightning Source LLC
LaVergne TN
LVHW050206080826
844660LV00012B/366

* 9 7 8 0 8 1 3 2 2 5 1 1 1 *